Coaching from the Inside

Coaching from the Inside

The Guiding Principles of Internal Coaching

J. Val Hastings

Open University Press

Open University Press
McGraw Hill
8th Floor, 338 Euston Road
London
England
NW1 3BH

email: enquiries@openup.co.uk
world wide web: www.openup.co.uk

First edition published 2021

Copyright © Open International Publishing Limited, 2021

A catalogue record of this book is available from the British Library

ISBN-13: 9780335249794
ISBN-10: 0335249794
eISBN: 9780335249800

Library of Congress Cataloging-in-Publication Data
CIP data applied for

Typeset by Transforma Pvt. Ltd., Chennai, India

Praise page

"*I met Val Hastings when I started coaching. He was already a Master Coach and I was just beginning my practice. Nonetheless, he took me by the hand and brought me to also being a Master Coach myself. More than an impeccable technical mentor and teacher, he is a generous and true person that really believes in what he does and really believes in people. His books and trainings are the result of a creative and skilled professional that manages to brilliantly explain complex concepts in a tangible and accessible way. Internal coaching – or coaching granted from the inside of any organization – is a true challenge due to the relationships and conflicts of interest that could take place. Only a masterful and insightful coach as Val Hastings could put together a book which teaches how to really deal with this scenario. This one is to be studied once, twice... again, again and again.*"

Juliana de Lacerda Camargo, Master Certified Coach, Partner of R122 and Representative of C4TL in Brazil

"*Val shares stories and insights from people across the world who are using coaching inside their organisations. This book will enable you to make your own meaning about what coaching from the inside might be like where you work and lead. Val shares some great insights and ideas on changing the culture of organisations so that colleagues listen more than they fix.* Coaching from the Inside *makes transformation more accessible for everyone!*"

Claire Pedrick MCC, Author of Simplifying Coaching

"*Dr. Val Hastings offers 'eleven guiding principles' to lead from the inside to develop diverse and inclusive leadership in organizations and businesses. Based on the collective wisdom of experienced internal coaches, Hastings provides how to coach the system that will produce sustainable results.* Coaching from the Inside *is a masterpiece that reminds leaders that it will bring out the best in individuals, teams, and organizations when developing a coaching culture. The person-focused internal coaching leadership will bring organizational excellence to the next level of success.*"

HiRho Y. Park, PhD., DMin., PCC, Vice President for International Relations and Advancement, Huree University, Mongolia

It is a great joy to read and recommend Coaching from the Inside *by Dr. J. Val Hastings. Val has been training internal coaches for our California-Pacific Annual Conference of the United Methodist Church for the last 5 years, and over 200 of our own coaches have gone through his program. His latest book on internal coaching provides powerful insights and suggestions on individual coaching, team coaching and the systems with which internal coaches have to work with. It is masterfully written and a must-read for all coaches!*

Bishop Grant Hagiya, Resident Bishop of the California-Pacific Annual Conference of The United Methodist Church

Contents

Preface

On my first day of kindergarten I found myself standing behind the classroom piano, being punished for drawing a picture that was too big. Let me explain. We were asked to draw a picture of what we wanted to do when we grew up. My drawing was so big that I ended up drawing on my desk and on the other children's papers. Before putting me behind the piano, my teacher scolded me saying, "You can't draw such big pictures. You're going to have to learn to stay on your own paper."

Don't worry, I wasn't traumatized or scarred for life from my teacher's words. I quickly shook off the scolding and continued drawing and thinking big. Decades later I get a good laugh out of that memory.

My introduction to coaching was much like my first day of kindergarten. My initial experience of being coached was nothing short of a "wow" experience. In addition to feeling like someone was tapping into my inner—somewhat hidden—greatness, I immediately caught a vision of *every leader a coach!* I knew instantly that it wasn't enough for me to be coached and to coach others, I also wanted to be part of a global movement that trained others to coach and equipped coaches with the best possible resources.

Over the past twenty years I have developed several coach training programs accredited by the Internal Coaching Federation. In addition, I have written numerous books and even presented at the global gathering of the International Coaching Federation (ICF) in 2006.

I have also had the unique privilege of training and mentoring thousands of coaches for their ACC, PCC, and MCC coaching credentials, and I am an assessor of these credentials for the ICF.

I have facilitated internal coaching programs for numerous organizations, corporations, and associations. I've watched as these internal coaching programs tipped to become a culture of coaching.

Our training program has been translated into five different languages, and most years I have traveled to five continents personally delivering coach training. And you guessed it, my sights are set to train on six to seven continents in a year!

This book is a compilation of my twenty years of coaching experience, along with that of twenty-one other internal coaches from around the world. Over the years I have found that coaches are quick to share their experiences and wisdom with others, and the same was true with those I interviewed. Without hesitation they shared their insights, stories, and struggles as internal coaches. My vision is that this book will be a resource that will better equip you as a coach, while driving forward my vision of *every leader a coach.*

Why this book?

There aren't many dedicated resources for internal coaches, though this is the largest growing sector of coaches internationally.

Internal coaching in the global community is rapidly rising among for-profit and not-for-profit organizations. Faith communities, educational institutions, twelve-step programs, small businesses, helping organizations, governmental departments, and global corporations are all seeing the value of coaching and are launching internal coaching cohorts.

The 2020 ICF Global Coaching Study, commissioned by the International Coaching Federation and undertaken by PricewaterhouseCoopers, LLP, surveyed coach practitioners and managers and leaders using coaching skills from around the world. Along with current and past members of the ICF, members of other professional coaching bodies as well as business and professional organizations were invited to participate, including:

- Association for Talent Development (ATD)
- Human Capital Institute (HCI) and Society for Human Resource Management (SHRM)
- Association for Coaching (AC)
- Association of Coach Training Organizations (ACTO)
- European Mentoring and Coaching Council (EMCC)
- Graduate School Alliance for Executive Coaching (GSAEC)
- International Association of Coaching (IAC)
- World Business and Executive Coach Summit (WBECS).

The study's executive summary offers the following survey results:

- Globally, it is estimated that there were approximately 71,000 coach practitioners in 2019, an increase of 33% on the 2015 estimate. Growth was especially strong in the emerging regions of Latin America and the Caribbean (+174%) and Eastern Europe (+40%).
- The number of managers/leaders using coaching skills is estimated to have risen by almost half (+46%). This estimate should be viewed as strictly indicative and subject to a higher level of uncertainty than the figures for coach practitioners. However, similar to the coach practitioner estimates, Latin America and the Caribbean recorded the largest growth (+198%). In Asia, the estimated number of managers/leaders using coaching skills more than doubled (+124%).
- A little under one in five coach practitioners (17%) work as both an internal and external coach practitioner. On average, they devote a higher proportion of their time to their internal coaching practice (54%).
- Almost all coach practitioners (94%) offer services in addition to coaching. Most frequently, coach practitioners also offer consulting (60%), training (60%), and/or facilitation services (54%).
- There has been a sharp rise among managers/leaders using coaching skills in the strength of agreement that clients expect their coaches to be certified/credentialed. The proportion of respondents who strongly agree rose from 37% in 2015 to 55% in 2019.

- The proportion of managers/leaders with 200 or more hours of coach training varies widely by region, from 39% in Latin America and the Caribbean to 14% in the Middle East and Asia.
- Almost three in four managers/leaders (74%) said they plan to enroll in additional coach-specific training in the next 12 months.
- Among those planning to enroll in additional training, a little over one in two (52%) said they wanted to enhance their coaching skills. The remaining 48% said they wanted to become a coach practitioner, with most intending to become a hybrid external and internal coach practitioner.

While we are seeing huge leaps and bounds in the launch of internal coaching, what is lagging behind is the development of internal coaching resources. For example, a search of coaching books revealed a preponderance of texts about external coaching, with very few pertaining to internal coaching.

There was also a similar shortfall in training options for internal coaches. The coaches I interviewed said that when they did attend coach training programs and coaching events, the experience frequently fell short—not really addressing the internal coach's world or experience.

The 2020 ICF Global Coaching Study: Executive Summary reported the top three potential obstacles to building a strong coaching culture inside an organization were:

- Limited support from senior leaders (50%)
- Inability to measure impact of coaching (42%)
- Lack of budget for coaching activities (38%).

Why I was called to write this book

Over the past few years I have noticed a dramatic increase in the number of our coach training students already in, or moving toward, an internal coach position. Simultaneously, I have noted a dramatic increase in leaders wanting to develop a coaching culture within their organization.

Organizational leaders are seeing a coaching culture as an environment where employees and members have an internal desire to contribute and self-manage, i.e., they behave like owners of the company.

I have also seen that those planning on becoming internal coaches have a different set of needs and questions than external coaches. For example:

- How do you manage potential conflicts of interest?
- How do you coach when you have a vested interest in the outcome?
- What practical suggestions would you offer regarding the various roles of the internal coach?
- How do you seamlessly shift hats (change roles) as an internal coach?
- Who are we really in service of?

- How do I help leaders understand what coaching is, as well as its value to the organization?
- How do I help the top-tier leaders within my organization understand the value of coaching?
- How do you coach the system?

More and more of our coach training students are coming from the internal coach environment and I wanted to learn more about internal coaches so that our training program could tailor our approach to internal coaches.

Being an external coach myself, I knew I'd need to draw on the experience of established internal coaches to answer these questions.

The interview process

I was aiming for a representation of a wide geographic area throughout North America, South America, Asia, and Europe, including Canada, the US, Brazil, the UK, the Ukraine, Amsterdam, and South Korea. Some of these coaches in turn passed along the questionnaire to their colleagues in still other locations.

I was also seeking coaches working in a variety of industries, including non-profit, large corporations, and government agencies. Most, if not all, of these coaches initially had other roles in that workplace and then transitioned to an internal coaching role.

In my request, I offered for each person to either write out their answers to my questions, or to have a video or telephone chat where we would talk through the questions together.

By the end of the process, I had interviewed twenty-one coaches, resulting in sixteen interview transcriptions and five written responses. I conducted a telephone interview with an additional coach about one specific topic that was not recorded or transcribed.

Interviews were framed around the following ten questions:

1   What is your professional background (training, credentials, etc.)?
2   How, when, and why did you become an internal coach?
3   What is your specialty as a coach/internal coach?
4   Tell us more about where you work.
5   What are some stories or examples that you can share about your experiences as an internal coach?
6   What are some of the best practices and other insights you can share with other internal coaches?
7   If you were to create a training program specifically for internal coaches, what should absolutely be included? What do you wish you had known as a new internal coach?
8   What do you feel is unique about internal coaching?

9   Do you have any warnings about missteps or misunderstandings to avoid?

10   What else would be helpful to share with other internal coaches?

In the written responses, coaches answered some or all of the questions, depending on their individual experiences and available time.

In the telephone and video interviews, conversations—similar to coaching conversations—veered in different directions, often leading to new and exciting discoveries that changed the trajectory of the book.

Introduction

What is internal coaching?

First, it's important to understand that internal coaching is coaching—100% coaching, no questions asked! Internal coaches, similar to external coaches, believe that their clients are healthy, whole, and creative. That means that the internal coach can lean heavily on the experience and expertise of their clients, rather than their own expertise. Both internal and external coaches focus on tapping into the greatness of their clients by *asking*, rather than demonstrating their own brilliance by *telling*.

During many of the interviews that I conducted with internal coaches, I heard coaches almost apologetically commenting that they didn't feel as though they were 100% coaches by the standards of the International Coaching Federation. Each time I would say, "No need to apologize. What you offer as an internal coach is every bit coaching."

What I did observe, though, was a more frequent and responsive shift in and out of coach mode. Many internal coaches referred to this as switching hats from coach to consultant to trainer and so on. Viktor Glinka commented that switching roles is a challenge for internal coaches because you don't work only as an internal coach.

I also observed differences in how the core coaching competencies compared to what I have observed in external coaches. For example, I observed that direct communication was used more frequently and earlier in the internal coaching process than when coaching externally. Successful internal coaches also very quickly develop a mastery of on-the-spot coaching.

Internal coaching operates from within the organization and frequently employs coaches who are already part of the organization. Compare and contrast this to external coaching, which takes place outside of the organization where the coach is also outside of the organization.

Already a part of the system, the internal coach frequently has a relational history with their client and knows the individuals and teams that are referenced during the coaching conversation. The internal coach is not only within the system, they are also part of the system. The latter is most significant and will be addressed later in this book.

What are the unique differences between internal and external coaching?

1   As the internal coach, you have the opportunity to see and experience the system firsthand, and your client's place in that system. Rachel Silva notes, "You have the ability to stay longer and see the fruits of coaching. See the

organization and people change over time. Also having the feeling and the empathy to understand the environmental challenges people face in their daily lives. [You can] build bonds, good relationships, and the trust needed to better succeed. As an external coach, you are usually receiving second-hand information about the system from your client."

2   As an internal coach, you are in the system and have a vested interest in the outcome of the coaching. As an external coach, your primary interest is the success of your client and there is little to no investment outside of their success.

3   As an internal coach, you are doing multidirectional/multidimensional coaching (e.g., upward coaching, peer coaching, performance coaching, systems coaching, individual, intact team coaching). As an external coach, you are primarily doing unidirectional/unidimensional coaching.

4   Internal coaching happens in the moment. As you and your clients go about daily work routines, coaching happens. As an external coach, your coaching is primarily scheduled.

5   As an internal coach, the reward and risk factors are much higher when being brave and bold (we call this "skinny branch coaching"); you risk losing everything since all of your clients are within the same organization. As an external coach, skinny branch coaching still requires being brave and bold, but the worst-case scenario is that you only lose a single client or organization out of your total caseload.

6   As an internal coach, you need to become fluent in the non-verbal language and cultural norms of your organization (e.g., habits, patterns, and unspoken assumptions that guide decisions), primarily because you are living and working on a daily basis in this environment. As the external coach, you rely heavily on the fluency of your clients to inform you and the coaching.

7   As an internal coach, you know the players in your workplace, and you have a history that is part of the coaching. Syed Ali shared, "You have a long-term relationship with teams and leaders. People have more trust and you have more insights about organizational strategic goals. As an external coach, you are once removed from the players and history and are relying on your client's commentary of the players."

8   As an internal coach, contracting agreements are multidimensional (one-to-many) and you need to be alert to inevitable conflicts of interest. As an external coach, the majority of your contracts are uni- or bi-directional (one-to-one or one-to-two).

9   Internal coaches are often working alongside other internal coaches within the same organization. Syed Ali suggests that internal coaches must work together as a team to improve sustainability and consistency among the teams.

My interviews suggest that internal coaches often feel like a second cousin of the coaching family. They find it difficult to identify other internal coaches when they participate in larger coaching gatherings, and the coach gatherings they have attended have frequently failed to address or inform the internal coaching world.

What do internal coaches need that they aren't getting from existing resources designed for external coaches?

Many of those I interviewed unknowingly backed into coaching. Their path to coaching was not a straight line, instead often a zig-zag path of new discoveries. For many, the formal introduction to the core coaching skills came later, rather than sooner.

A recurring need I heard from these internal coaches was for a solid introduction to the core coaching skills. This includes opportunities to practice coaching skills in scenarios that are relevant to their setting, and to get informed feedback.

Some of these scenarios could include designing triangle coaching agreements, dealing with multiple overlapping agreements when coaching within a system, and asking questions when you are part of the system. Internal coaches would also benefit from practical skill development as to how to switch hats while coaching, and using assessments and other tools during coaching.

Many internal coaches expressed a desire for ongoing peer coaching done in a triad setting of coach, client, and observer. These coaching triads would meet several needs:

- An opportunity to be coached
- An opportunity to coach and receive peer feedback
- An opportunity to observe coaching.

"Coaches need more frequent feedback," says Viktor, who also thinks internal coach training should start with participants answering questions like, "Why do I want to be a coach? Why is it important for me to be a coach? What person do I need to be to be a great coach? And what do I already have to be a great coach?"

Learning how to establish yourself as a coach is also very different as an internal coach. Many assume that internal coaches do not need to demonstrate their worth, or the value of coaching. As I discovered in my interviews, demonstrating your worth as an internal coach is of the uppermost importance, both to your immediate supervisors and to the larger organization.

During my interviews, I also heard many internal coaches speak about the importance of healthy self-care, especially when you are coaching from within the system and have a stake in the outcome. Christine Thompson emphasized the importance of recognizing personal triggers, the need for boundaries, and self-differentiation from the organization. Others suggested assigning a coach to each student coach right from the start, to ensure self-care and skill development.

Several internal coaches also expressed a desire to connect with the larger coaching community after graduation and certification. Many of the agile coaches that I interviewed shared about the benefits of being connected with other agile coaches around the world. Other internal coaches expressed a desire to be connected to the large coaching community.

How can you get the best experience from reading/using this book?

If you are new to coaching, I'd encourage you to read this book from cover to cover. I have intentionally designed this book with two audiences in mind: the coaching novice and the experienced coach. This chapter and "A case for coaching," which follows, will really enrich the knowledge and resources of the novice coach. The balance of the book will be beneficial to both novice and experienced coaches.

The core section of this book contains the guiding principles of internal coaching, and is filled with the knowledge and expertise of the internal coaches that I interviewed. It will provide you with helpful insights and approaches to internal coaching and creating a coaching culture.

Definitions and distinctions

The following definitions and distinctions will be helpful as you read this book:

Mentoring	Supervision	Coaching
• Advice-based • Expert to non-expert • Mentor-directed • Advice and support focus	• Improvement-based • Expert to non-expert • Supervisor-directed • Instruction and improvement focus • Fill gaps and address needs • Overall responsibility rests with the supervisor	• Process-based • Expert to expert • Client-directed • Discovery and developmental focus • Coach is thinking partner • Overall responsibility rests with the client

Individual coaching	Team coaching	Group coaching
• Individual focus • Coaching dependent on the self-reporting of the client • Process-based: assumes the client has what they need within themselves • The coaching work belongs to the individual	• Collective focus • Relationships, roles, and history are already in existence and sustained after coaching • Coaching is dependent on the collective reporting • Process-based: assumes the team has what they need within themselves • The coaching work belongs to the collective	• Individual focus within a group • Relationships may or may not be in existence prior to coaching. Relationships are usually not sustained after coaching • The coaching is dependent on the self-reporting of the client, while being influenced and informed by others in the group • Process-based: assumes that each individual has what they need within themselves and this is accelerated by a listen-and-learn approach. • The coaching work belongs to the individual

Systems coaching

- Organizational focus
- Multidimensional and multidirectional relationships, roles, and history are already in existence and sustained after coaching
- The coaching is dependent on the collective reporting, both vertically and horizontally within the organization
- Process-based: assumes the system has what they need within themselves
- The coaching work belongs to the organization

Manager as coach/Leader as coach

- Coaching within an organization
- Already have a prior role within the organization, other than coaching
- Manage multiple roles in addition to coaching; coaching is one of many responsibilities
- Coaching is both scheduled and spontaneous – *in the moment*
- Primarily process-based; content-based as needed

Internal coaching	External coaching	Agile coaching

• Coaching within an organization
• Manage multiple relationships
• Relationships include:
  o Sponsor: this is who advocates for funding for the coaching and is responsible for bringing you inside the organization. This may or may not be an HR person
  o HR and L/D: this is who you relate to in an ongoing manner. They provide you with valuable information, including: definitions of success, strategic initiatives and the overall vision and direction of the larger organization. They are also your advocate
	• Coaching various individuals, teams, groups representing many organizations.
	• The relationship is typically one or two parties, including your client and there may also be a payee or sponsor.
	• Coaching is typically scheduled.
	• Primarily process-based. Content-based as needed.
		• More than coaching within an organization: coaching, training, mentoring, and facilitation
		• Manage multiple relationships
		• Coaching is both scheduled and spontaneous – *in the moment*
		• Uses both process-based (coaching and facilitation) and content-based (teaching and mentoring) skillsets
		• It's a one-to-many model

- o Your clients: teams, groups, and individuals
- o Your client's supervisor or manager
- o Other internal coaches within the organization
- o Organizational decision-makers
- Coaching is both scheduled and spontaneous – *in the moment*
- Primarily process-based; content-based as needed
- It's a one-to-many model

- Typical model is one-to-one or one-to-two

1 A case for coaching

What is coaching and why should you care?

In 1999 I met my first coach. I attended a training event and sat next to a very tall woman. The facilitator of the training event introduced himself and then invited us to introduce ourselves to each other. The tall woman sitting next to me introduced herself as Fontelle and told me that she was a coach. I asked her what sport she coached. She laughed and proceeded to introduce me to the world of coaching. Before the day was over, I had scheduled my first-ever coaching session. Over the next several months I met with Fontelle, my coach, and experienced firsthand the benefits of coaching.

There's another side to this story. While I was intrigued by coaching, I was also skeptical and wondered if it really worked. Prior to my first coaching session, I decided that I wouldn't tell anyone that I was being coached – except my wife. After about three months of coaching, the team that evaluated my professional work asked to meet with me. This was an unplanned, unscheduled meeting, which usually isn't a good sign.

During the meeting they asked what I was doing differently. I think my confused reaction to their question prompted them to say, "You seem much more relaxed and focused than usual. Your communication, which is usually very good, has also improved. We have been noticing a difference and wanted to tell you that whatever you are doing, keep doing it." It was then that I told them that I had been working with a coach. I also told them that I was considering learning how to coach. They unanimously agreed and made it possible for me to begin my coach training.

Shortly after this impromptu meeting I began wondering what my coach had done during those coaching sessions that prompted this noticeable change in me. As I reviewed our coaching conversations, I noted that she had done a lot of listening. I mean a lot! And when she did speak, she usually asked me a question. Most of her questions I couldn't answer right away. The biggest thing I recalled, though, was that she hadn't tried to fix me. Instead, she drew things out of me and I came up with my own answers. That was the beginning of developing my own definition of coaching.

The coaches that I interviewed for this book shared with me not only the benefits of coaching for those that they coach, they also shared the benefits they experienced when they were coached themselves. Allison Pollard said that she drills this idea into new coaches, asking, "Who coaches you? Who are your support people?"

These two questions arise from her personal experience of wanting to practice self-care, yet having recurring moments of self-reflection where she recognizes she's not doing it as well as she thought.

Erkan Kadir notes that since people see the internal coach on a day-to-day basis, how you show up will matter. You want to show up in a way that really encourages them to want to work with you. This is another reason that the internal coach needs to have their own coach.

Geertruyt Stokes shared how important coaching and coaching supervision have been for her. As an internal coach you may be working within an unhealthy system, where a lot of blaming goes on. It's easy for the internal coach to get caught up in this, and working with a coach will really help.

Kathy Sauve, another internal coach I interviewed for this book, describes how her co-workers responded when she first introduced them to coaching: "'Usually, you go to an event and they teach you a skill, and you get this library of skills.' This was different, they said. It was about taking the skills that you already have and using them to live life under pressure. It was about living when life's hard—both professionally and personally."

Over the past several years, Kathy has continued to provide her co-workers with coaching and coach training. She offers an open and shut case for coaching when she says, "I think an organization that doesn't have internal coaching is never going to make the most of its people," and that having better people equals having better leaders.

In making his own case for coaching, Vernon Stinebaker says that with traditional training, so much is lost. "People, they're just kind of drinking from a fire hose, so to speak. And the human brain is not really designed effectively to do that. And so now, most of my focus is on a longer-term, more integrated learning. And predominantly learner-driven learning. And coaching is a great fit for that."

During my interview with internal coach Christine Thompson, I asked her to state the case for internal coaching. In other words, why would an organization have a team of internal coaches on their payroll? Here's how she responded:

"Imagine having somebody in-house who can support people when they need it, who can help people to become more self-sufficient, more empowered, more motivated, more successful in what they do. What's the value of that? So for each of these individuals that you can support and move forward, you're going to get a more effective, more efficient business, rather than employees who are demotivated, sitting back, unhappy, just don't know what to do about it. That's a huge value.

And it's not only people, is it? It's departments, the whole lot. It's more than just working with the individuals because it's also the coaching training, it's helping other people. I've worked in my previous organization to train the managers to coach. So they are actually learning the skills for themselves. I mean, they're not going to learn deep coaching skills, but they're going to learn ways of having more effective conversations with people.

And that also is adding value because it means when people are going to their one-to-one chats with their manager, they're getting more value out of that conversation, because their manager is having a coaching conversation rather than a, 'You need to do this, and if you don't, I'll beat you with a stick,' conversation. It's making the whole organization more effective and more supported by actually passing those skills onto the people as well.

You're creating a coach culture, which is what is part of what I call modern leadership. It comes with a coaching mindset. So it goes away from the days when managers came and told everybody what to do, and they did it. This is about helping people to help themselves. And coming from that mindset, when you're working with teams, you're going to get much better results. So yes, it's creating that mindset across the whole organization.

So the investment of having one or more internal coaches, for the salary that you're going to pay that person, the improved efficiency and motivation and outcomes that you're going to get from the work of that one person, seriously offsets what you're paying for their salary. And also, you pay less for an internal coach than you pay for an external coach. It just seems to me that it's worth that investment to make a difference to the business on an ongoing basis."

Coaching definitions and models

Some of you reading this book know what coaching is, primarily because you have either worked with a coach or you are a coach. Others, though, I suspect, are like me in 1999, wondering what coaching is and if it's something for you to consider.

I'm really glad that my introduction to coaching wasn't a textbook definition or an elevator speech about coaching. I believe that the best way to know what coaching is, and if it's right for you, is to be coached. Offering a complimentary introductory coaching session is standard practice in our profession. If a coach won't offer you a complimentary session before you begin coaching, then that coach isn't worth giving a second thought. During your coaching session you will experience what I did many years ago, and you will see firsthand the value of regular coaching conversations.

If you would like a complimentary coaching session, please consider one of the coaches that I have interviewed for this book, or contact me. We have a number of students and graduates from our coach training program that are always looking for someone to coach.

Three of my favorite definitions of coaching are:

1 I help people move from good to great
2 I shorten the learning curve
3 Coaching builds a bridge between where you are and where you want to be.

Implied in all of my definitions is that the person is basically healthy and whole. Coaching is not about fixing. Instead, coaching is about developing and drawing out the very best in the other person. As Vernon says, "believing that our clients are resourceful and creative and capable, and so really giving them a support structure as needed, or helping them create their own support structures. But really letting them drive and develop around their own interests and their own challenges."

Many of today's helping professionals (therapists, consultants, and mentors) have been trained to focus on what is wrong, broken, and flawed in their clients. The coach focuses on what is great about the person. What are their strengths, gifts, and passions? Coaches are trained to follow the positive energy during a coaching conversation. A conversation that focuses on fixing is markedly different from one that focuses on strengths and greatness.

The coaching relationship is expert-to-expert

Many of today's helping professionals adopt an expert-to-non-expert relationship. Coaching, taking a page from renowned therapist Carl Rogers, believes that the patient (client) is the expert. In coaching the relationship is expert-to-expert. Our belief is that the people we coach, because they are basically healthy and whole, are the experts of their own lives.

Yes, the coach also has expertise as a result of their coach training, other professional expertise, and life experiences. Hence the coaching conversation is one that is expert-to-expert—with the coach intentionally holding back on their expertise and only sharing expertise when it empowers and benefits the other.

Pradeepa Narayanaswamy stresses that we need to continuously help people understand what coaching is. She'll hear executives make jokes or comments that show they still have this "iffy belief" about coaching, like, "Oh, who's our next victim for coaching?" This tells her she needs to have a conversation with them as to why coaching is not a punishment, why coaching can be a gift, right, and why language matters. Because if people hear that, "Oh, who's the next victim?," then they will go into the coaching thinking that they are a victim to it.

She finds there is also still a huge misunderstanding about how coaching is different from therapy:

> "I always go back to saying, 'I don't see anything is broken with you. I don't see anything is wrong with you. I see you as a whole person. I see you as a creative person. I see you. You can dig deeper into your creative intelligence. And your wisdom is going to trump any of my good answers for you. I trust your wisdom.' I have to re-repeat that over and over again just so that people hear me and say, 'Oh, this is different, because this is not therapy.'"

Coaching and the theater stage

Another useful metaphor for coaching is that of the theater stage. Matt Bloom, PhD of the Well Being at Work Project at the University of Notre Dame speaks of the leader being "on stage" when doing their work, and being "off stage" when away from their work. He then reminds us of the third stage, which he calls the "backstage."

In the theater, a significant amount of time, energy, and preparation is devoted to the work that goes on backstage. Feedback, movement, trust, and timing are all key components backstage.

The backstage of leadership is where things are coordinated and come together. This is where vital, honest feedback is offered. Trust is a key component backstage. The backstage to leadership is the primary work of the coach.

Consider the following backstage questions:

- Who is truthful with you, as leader, about what's really happening?
- Who do I trust enough to be challenged by what they say?
- Do you have enough of the right kind of backstage supervision for the work that you do and the influence you have on the lives of others?

Train people how to use coaching

If you are considering developing an internal coaching focus in your organization, you will need to do more than simply make a case for coaching. You will also need to train people how to use you as a coach. Christine says that in the work setting, people aren't used to having someone listen to them—not to fix them but to develop them.

In a corporate setting that's often focused on tasks, strategies, visions, outcomes, goals, and the bottom line, the coach is the human side. Coaching is where people can say, "Here's what I'm feeling," and "Here's what I'm struggling with." Even in the nonprofit realm where you're dealing with people's souls and spirits, when you're working toward cultural change and—again—that bottom line, the human touch is just as much a soft spot.

Internal coach Geertruyt shares a similar message that the company needs to be trained. Things to consider include: Who all needs to be aware? Who all needs to be trained? What's the story here? What's the story of me doing this work, and why is the company willing to pay for this? You will also want to get active systemic support, she says, so that they will introduce you and speak well of you, that they will tell you, "Please come to my management team and coach me," so that they model this for others.

Don't just be catapulted into the company and then have to sort it out yourself; that's a recipe for disaster. Harris Christopoulos says that often the internal coach, when they first arrive at a company, is perceived as the messiah. The coach will solve all the company's problems, but in the way that the company already has in mind. Geertruyt suggests internal coaches sit down with HR, be clear about what your role is and isn't, and get their support.

Madhavi Ledalla says that when an organization launches an internal coaching program they have high hopes on us. We, as internal coaches, tend to get into the consulting mode because we want to give solutions and we want to ensure that things are showing the results quickly. Resist this urge and stay in true coach mode.

Once you have officially launched your internal coaching effort, you will have to make the case for coaching over and over again. A recurring theme among those that I interviewed was the need to routinely demonstrate your worth and communicate the value that you bring to the company.

Richard Lister refers to the internal coach as storyteller, citing this as one of the essential roles of the internal coach. As the storyteller, you will need to communicate the stories of your coaching and the impact it is having. You will also need to teach your clients how to communicate to their supervisor the value that your coaching brings to the organization. We will focus much more specifically on this in the section about the guiding principle of demonstrating your worth.

In addition to training people how to use you as a coach, it is also very helpful to provide basic coaching skills to the leaders within the organization. This not only equips them with helpful skills, it also improves the actual coaching that you do with them.

Imagine a workplace environment in which a growing number of people were actually listening—deeply! How different our interactions would be if we related to each other as expert-to-expert. The health and forward movement of an organization could grow exponentially in a coaching culture. In addition, with their newfound coaching skills, your clients can coach themselves before and after each coaching session. In many cases this pre- and post-session self-coaching will provide an opportunity for the coaching conversation between coach and client to go much deeper.

2 Meet the coaches

When I asked those I interviewed how they got into coaching, several common themes emerged. One was that many internal coaches "backed into" coaching. Coaching was not on their radar. They were asked to become internal coaches and functioned in that capacity, sometimes only years later deciding to pursue coach training.

For most internal coaches, ICF-accredited coach training and coaching certification are a fairly new phenomenon. Most of those I interviewed either recently received an ICF coaching credential or had received some level of accredited coach training.

Another common theme was that almost all of the internal coaches were already working within the organization where they eventually became an internal coach. Several were initially invited to a variety of training events, which later introduced them to coaching.

A common driver among all of those I interviewed was the pursuit of excellence, and a common trait was a commitment to continuous learning and skill development.

Meet the coaches

Here are the coaches, with each telling the story of how they got started in internal coaching:

Alex Sloley from Sydney, NSW, Australia

The first thing that I noticed during my interview with Alex was his accent. More specifically, his lack of an Australian accent. When I asked him about it, he told me about the great adventure that he and his family embarked on in 2015 when he was recruited to do an agile transformation in Australia. Alex and his family saw this as an adventure that took them from Seattle, Washington to Sydney, Australia. In addition to hearing his wisdom on internal coaching, Alex shared several of his adventures in Australia.

Alex has a solid handle of the agile world, including agile coaching. During the course of our interview, he explained the agile world to me and shared numerous resources. I was most appreciative of the distinction that Alex made between coaches being agents of change versus agents of awareness. This distinction was so important that, as you will discover, being agents of awareness became one of the guiding principles of internal coaching.

How did Alex get started in internal coaching?

"I discovered a new passion that I decided I couldn't live without anymore—helping other people succeed. So I sought out other people who had similar interests and started making friends, learning new things, and attending workshops, trainings, and conferences. And then one day I found a post online about the first ever Scrum Alliance Agile Coaching Retreat and a two-day workshop with Lyssa Adkins and Michael Spayd. I bought my tickets and my life changed afterwards. That was December 2011. Since then, I have dedicated myself to the craft of agile coaching and take pride and joy from knowing that I am doing what I always set out to do—help others."

Allison Pollard from Dallas/Ft. Worth, Texas, USA

One of the things that I really appreciate about Allison is that she has a firm grasp on systems coaching. At the start of our conversation, as well as throughout, she offered commentary on how to coach a system and why. I also appreciated the wealth of real stories and examples of systems coaching.

During our interview, she spoke of "catching them in the act," referring to the fact that internal coaches have the unique opportunity to observe our clients firsthand during their good days and their difficult days. She lit up as she shared how she has witnessed firsthand the amazing impact of coaching.

How did Allison get started in internal coaching?

"As I'd been learning about teams using agile methods, I met a local agile coach named Gary McCants. Whenever I felt stuck on a challenge with my development team, he helped me to see a new idea to try. One day I told Gary, 'I want your job.'

I wanted to visit different workplaces and help people with change. That jumpstarted my coaching journey. I joined the consulting company Gary worked for, and after a few months felt like there was something more I was missing in my work. A class on Coaching Agile Teams caught my eye, and I brought Lyssa Adkins and Michael Spayd to Dallas to teach it. They opened my eyes to professional coaching. It was the 'something' I'd been desiring."

Brock Argue from Calgary, Alberta, Canada

A conversation with Brock has to include an explanation of how he and his partner Erkan came up with the name of his company, Superheroes Academy. According to Brock, superheroes academy was the best URL that they could find. As the story continues, Brock also explained to me why he has a framed superman insignia on his office wall. During his childhood, Brock frequently wore a superman costume and the framed insignia is from a superman costume that his mom made for him many years ago.

While no longer an internal coach, Brock spoke with me from the space of when he was an internal coach, as well as what he has learned from being a coaching consultant. Brock's two-pronged perspective prompted him to say that as an internal coach, "You've got to help them help you!"—referring to immediate supervisors who see firsthand the value of coaching, yet struggle with how to communicate this with upper management and decision-makers.

How did Brock get started in internal coaching?

"My journey to become an internal coach started as a mid-level manager in a software company in Calgary, Canada. I had been in management for about two years when the company was acquired by a much larger global enterprise. The new organization introduced many management training programs—one of which I consider the start of my coaching journey. The three pivotal events in my journey to become an internal coach were:

- Attending a management training event focused on emotional intelligence. I learned that I lacked self-awareness and underwent a process to grow in this area. Key individuals: my manager and my father.

- Qualifying for the Certified Enterprise Coach (CEC) designation through the Scrum Alliance. I learned what gaps existed in my coaching and developed connections with amazing coaches in the agile space. Key individuals: two CEC mentors from the Scrum Alliance.

- Attending an agile coaching certification program. This program emphasized the necessity of professional coaching in agile organizations and was my first exposure to professional coaching. I started practicing one-on-one coaching and sought out training in systems coaching and vertical development coaching."

Cherie Silas from Dallas, Texas, USA

Cherie has the distinction of being the only MCC (Master Certified Coach) that I interviewed for this book. Cherie is both a master of coaching, and a master of internal coaching—especially all things agile. I really appreciated Cherie's willingness to share with me in great detail her approach to coaching systems, which she teaches in her coach training program, Tandem Coaching Academy.

I was taken aback with Cherie's candid assessment of a 98% failure rate with systemic coaching. A significant portion of this failure is due to the failure of demonstrating the worth of coaching to upper-tier leadership.

How did Cherie get started in internal coaching?

"My road to being an internal coach started as an executive leader who adopted a servant leadership model as a way of working with my staff. I had great passion for seeing others grow and become successful beyond the position they had with me.

From this full-time position I shifted to a consulting role (agile coach) helping companies adopt new ways of working and managing the flow of work throughout the company. When working with a rather large client that had very complex problems, I began to realize that consulting was not what they needed because I didn't know the individual domains well enough to give the best solutions.

So, I shifted to be more question-oriented to allow them to solve their own problems. After seeing how this worked so well, only then did I set out to get training and discover how to become a competent coach. While this road may seem very backwards, in the industry I am in it is generally the norm."

Christine Thompson from Maidenhead, Berkshire, UK

Christine and I hit it off from the very beginning, partly because we shared the opinion that the further north you go in the UK, the harder it is to understand the language. We had a good laugh about our common experiences of the English language spoken in the north of the UK.

It was remarkable for me to learn that Christine's professional journey toward becoming an internal coach began with a PhD in Molecular Biology. Mention the word coaching to Christine and very quickly you will experience her passion and conviction around coaching. Her own personal story of working with a coach, along with her firsthand experiences of coaching others, has made her a strong advocate for coaching—especially internal coaching.

How did Christine get started in internal coaching?

"Having worked as a Scrum Master for five years, two things contributed to my move towards an internal coaching role. The first of these was a personal development opportunity. Having suffered a period of stress at work, which resulted in an altercation with a colleague, my manager suggested that I consider taking an NLP practitioner training class.

This had a huge impact on my own mental state and opened my eyes to the possibility of helping develop people through coaching. Shortly after this, I spoke to a very experienced agile coach about where I might consider developing myself professionally. He introduced me to the idea of an ICF coaching program, which I later enrolled on. These two training experiences aligned to shape my new direction."

Claire Bamberg from Hartford, Connecticut, USA

Among those I interviewed, Claire is unique in that she brings a strong professional background in mental health and marriage and family therapy to internal coaching. Because of this, her slant on internal coaching is rather unique. While many internal coaches bring a toolkit filled with consulting, mentoring, and facilitation skills, Claire's toolkit includes therapy, psychology, and a family systems approach.

How did Claire get started in internal coaching?

"While working in my family's business was not my first job, it is the place where I learned to observe and work within systems, from the inside out.

My doctoral work was in mental health, and marriage and family therapy. There, I advanced what I had learned in life, named it, learned to draw it, and think—literally—in systems. As I began to work within various corporate systems (large and small) in the city in which I lived, I realized that systems dynamics were a part of every facet of these organizations. In 1991, I became known for that work, and was sought after wherever systems and relationships within those systems are not working well—efficiently or productively."

Doris Dalton from New York City, New York, USA

While new to coaching, Doris has quickly gained expertise as a coach. In her role as Director of Leadership Development and Intercultural Competency, she is connecting the dots between coaching and intercultural competency. She sees the direct connection between coaching skills and cultural competence, and is an advocate for coach training—having already trained a cohort of thirty coaches within her organization.

How did Doris get started in internal coaching?

"My personal mission statement is 'to extend the table of love so that all may eat and be full.' I joyfully embrace this calling by helping leaders live into their potential and purpose. My journey has included resource development, mentoring, teaching, and program development for leadership trainings.

In the early part of this journey, I discovered coaching as a resource for other leaders. I did not realize coaching was for me until recently, when I began to gather leaders to become trained coaches. For me, coaching is partnership in action, allowing me to walk alongside leaders as they make their journey towards their own brilliance."

Elise Shapiro from Seattle, Washington, USA

It's fascinating to me to hear the stories of the internal coaches I interviewed, in particular how they began their professional journey. Like many, Elise's professional journey did not begin with a focus on coaching or professional development. Hers began with a degree in art and five years as a photographer. While her journey began as a photographer, her frame of reference is the coaching mindset. A brief conversation with Elise would reveal her skill and expertise, which lead her early on to be invited into the agile world.

How did Elise get started in internal coaching?

"I got a degree in art, and I was a professional photographer for five years. And then I changed careers, and I began doing software administration and then technical program management for tech startups in San Francisco. From there, I kept being asked to be a Scrum Master, so I went back to school and learned how to do that.

Then, basically, Scrum Masters grow up to be agile coaches, and agile coaches, when they clue in to what's going on, figure out that they actually need to know how to actually coach. I was really strong in mentoring and facilitating and training but quite weak with the coaching skill. So five or six years ago I made that transition and trained as a coach, first with the Agile Coaching Institute, then with Coaches Training Institute, and then in a program called Positive Intelligence that's run by Shirzad Chamine, former CEO of CTI."

Erkan Kadir from Calgary, Alberta, Canada

Two things jumped out at me, prior to Erkan saying anything. One, the display of superhero action figures and insignias in his office. I later learned of his connection with Brock Argue and the Superheroes Academy. Second, a powerful question displayed on a whiteboard saying: "How often are you serving the organization?" As a collector of powerful questions, I frequently have a question on display.

During our forty-minute interview, Erkan shared a wealth of information about internal coaching, and especially agile coaching. Both Erkan and Brock reiterated during their interviews with me the importance of demonstrating your worth as a coach, citing that far too many coaches either ignore this topic or do not place enough emphasis on it.

How did Erkan get started in internal coaching?

"My story starts out as a manager in a software company that implemented agile methods. With the cornerstone of an agile company being self-organizing teams, all of a sudden, leaders such as myself were asked to check their expertise at the door and support those teams through coaching.

At first, it was challenging to give away power, but as I learned to step back and work through others, I noticed my teams succeeding and my impact at the company increasing. I owed it all to my new skill of coaching and dedicated my career to mastering the craft. It didn't take long for me to choose internal coaching full-time and I switched roles from Manager of Software Development to Director of Enterprise Coaching."

Geertruyt Stokes from Amsterdam, Netherlands

Geertruyt offered a unique perspective on internal coaching, focusing on the human side. She referred to internal coaching as the "soft spot" within the organization. Geertruyt stated, "You bring grace to the corporate work, where they're not used to a lot of grace." Throughout, she spoke to the human side of internal coaching. For example, she spoke about what you do with the information that you receive about other people within the organization. Another metaphor she offered was that as the soft spot within the organization, people will come to you like bees around a honey pot.

How did Geertruyt get started in internal coaching?

"I worked at a global consulting firm and our team was asked to educate the clients' employees in continuous improvement and coaching. The one client led to the other, and after a few years I trained over 100 internal coaches.

Although all coaches were connected to improvement programs, I trained them in the 'classic' ICF-style coaching, with a lot of emphasis on listening, asking questions, observing, letting the coachee do his or her own thinking, and balancing doing and being. Once the internal coaches got started, often as part of another full-time role, I provided supervision, peer-to-peer supervision, and ongoing education in the area of team coaching. I became a coach myself in the process."

Harris Christopoulos from Athens, Attiki, Greece

Harris gets the award for going the extra mile with his interview, as our interview took place from a Greek island during his holiday. My only regret was that it wasn't an in-person interview.

Much of our conversation focused on the importance of continuous learning for the internal coach. Harris is a strong advocate of triad coaching—even after graduation and certification. He also sees the real need for internal coaches to connect with coaches outside their organization, such as in communities of practice.

How did Harris get started in internal coaching?

"Having a technical background and after working for several years as an engineer in software development teams, I realized that I was more inclined to the human aspect of work. I was fascinated when there was a communication issue or an interpersonal challenge in a team to solve.

An influence for realizing that was the environment that I've been working in, a Scrum team embracing the values of the agile ways of working. Soon enough, I found myself spending more time reading topics about team dynamics, psychology, and human interactions rather than technical-related reading about my craft. As a result, taking over the role of an agile coach in a team and being certified as one were the stepping stones for the broader world of coaching in my professional career."

Kathy Sauve from Waterloo, Ontario, Canada

Kathy is a graduate of our coach training program and, as an internal coach, was one of the early students that asked questions unique to internal coaching. Kathy's questions provided me the much-needed nudge to further explore the internal coaching world and write this book.

During our interview, Kathy offered a distinction that I had never heard of before, that of advocate versus bridge. She explained to me that, as an internal coach, she did not see her role to be primarily that of an advocate for those she coached; instead, she saw her role to primarily be that of a bridge—making sure that people are hearing each other and bringing people together.

How did Kathy get started in internal coaching?

"I wanted to become a coach after experiencing it for myself. My coach helped me take those great ideas I had inside and apply them to a challenge I was experiencing. It was life-changing for me. As I was helping with leadership development, I invited her to lead a ten-week series. It was amazing to watch other leaders have a similar experience. One person summed it up well. He said, 'When I'm a better person, I'm a better leader.'

At the same time, I was using these coaching skills within my team. I had a good employee that was struggling. When I took a coaching approach, she told me that she felt really supported and was able to take responsibility for her growth. I knew then that I wanted to help build a coaching culture."

Madhavi Ledalla from Hyderabad, Telangana, India

Madhavi, an author herself, was eager to help with this book. Madhavi impressed upon me the unique position of the internal coach within an organization. Coaching from within the organization, you have unique knowledge of the organization and its internal culture that an external coach cannot access. Because of that, the internal coach can be a tremendous influencer of the organization. The internal coach has "reachability" because you are "one of us" within the organization.

I appreciated Madhavi's suggestion when beginning with a new organization. She encourages the coach to resist the urge to give quick solutions and show fast results. The organization has high hopes for you and it's tempting to skew into consulting or facilitating mode. Stay true to coaching! It will serve the organization best, in the long run.

How did Madhavi get started in internal coaching?

"My journey in agile started in the year 2008. The organization I was working for started its transformation journey and that was when I was formally introduced to agile. We were using Scrum to manage our projects, and I was playing the role of a Scrum Master. I got to experience how agile helps deal with complex problems in an empirical way. My Scrum Master journey reinforced my beliefs of how agile and Scrum can help deal with complex situations by allowing teams to course-correct at regular intervals.

I wanted to coach and teach Scrum to diverse teams and wanted to choose agile coaching as a career path. That is when I moved to an agile consulting role where I got the opportunity to work with diverse organizations. The only thing I could not experience as an external coach was to see how organizations and teams are able to sustain the journey in the long run. Consulting is usually short term in the sense that we develop internal coaches who are capable of leading their journeys and external coaches step out to help other organizations.

After having spent a significant amount of time offering services to clients as an external consultant, I transitioned to the role of an internal coach. The experience of being an internal coach is wholesome and the journey has been very fruitful so far."

Mauricio Robles from Costa Rica

The words that come to mind when I consider Mauricio are seasoned and solid. I heard in his contribution years of experience—success and the "school of hard knocks." For example, he encourages internal coaches to build a strong network within their organization. These will be the people that will support you with resources, and will be a strong advocate for coaching.

How did Mauricio get started in internal coaching?

"The path that took me to become an internal coach is tied with the events that got me started in my agile journey. While I was working for a small company of about 150 people, it was decided to get Scrum implemented. The CEO made the decision to have someone from inside trained and drive the implementation as a Scrum Master. Aside from my role, I was the go-to person when there was a problem with just about anything which I enjoyed.

As things evolved over time, I found myself with ten teams with their own Scrum Master and I learned two things that reshaped my role: I was no longer a Scrum Master of a team and I had to find a way for them to own the solution to their problems. At this point I realized that I had to start developing myself as an agile coach.

The 'internal' element was given by the fact that here in Costa Rica there aren't a lot of opportunities to go on as an external agile coach, so I focused on finding an organization that would provide opportunities to grow as a coach while providing stability."

Miriam Cheuk from Washington, DC, USA

While most of the internal coaches I interviewed did their coaching within a business or corporation, Miriam's setting was an educational system. As an instructional coach, Miriam emphasized the importance of relationships. "Everything you are doing, or not doing, on a daily basis is contributing to whether or not people will trust you." As a graduate of our coach training program, my experience of Miriam is that she is a master at developing relationships very quickly.

How did Miriam get started in internal coaching?

"Becoming an internal coach was not planned, as I've been a career educator at the secondary and university levels. While teaching at a secondary school in Virginia, my principal would send me teachers to coach/mentor unofficially. There, I also received a scholarship for a Masters in Educational Leadership from the school district. I felt that I was ready to take on a larger role!

Coincidentally, a new position of District Instructional Coach was created in 2007, and I was blessed to be chosen due to my experience and education. I continue to serve in that role and always look to refine my skills, like achieving the ICF PCC. I also offer life/leadership coaching outside my role at my school district."

Pauline Gallien from Houston, Texas, USA

Pauline, another internal coaching student in our program, routinely asked questions regarding internal coaching that I had never been asked before. What I appreciate about Pauline is that she didn't hesitate to answer the question that she had just asked.

Pauline is also one of those people that doesn't give up. She recounted in class that she was having difficulty conveying to the upper-tier leadership the value of coaching. So, she adopted another approach, deciding that at the next informal gathering of upper-tier leadership, she would adopt a coaching approach for the evening. The leaders were quite impressed with Pauline's "stealth" coaching and the tables soon turned in Pauline's favor.

How did Pauline get started in internal coaching?

"I always loved helping people achieve their potential, helping them become the best version of themselves. Bravely, I asked my HR leadership if they would support my pursuit of a coaching credential. They too, bravely, said yes.

After attending Val's Coaching 4 Today's Leaders and Marshall Goldsmith's Stakeholder Centered Coaching programs, I proposed our company conduct a beta test for internal coaching. In 2020, I got my first two senior leaders as coachees. In early 2021, we will add two more. In addition, a natural partnership has formed with our agile coaches in IT. Together, we have sponsored a coaching community of practice. Each month, over fifty current and aspiring leaders participate in the coaching community, both large and small groups.

Great things are happening!"

Pradeepa Narayanaswamy from Grapevine, Texas, USA

Pradeepa has a seemingly endless supply of stories from her time as an internal coach, each of them highlighting the benefits of internal coaching. Her stories also capture the significant benefits that she received, as the coach, while coaching others. For Pradeepa, there is mutual learning going on between the client and the coach, which results in growth for both.

How did Pradeepa get started in internal coaching?

"I got into coaching by accident. That's the best way that I can put it. I came from a technology background, first as a programmer, and then as a tester.

I was working as a development team member, with a little bit of a challenging team. After about six or seven months or so, colleagues told me the team was like night and day. Even though I was not a coach *per se*, they told me I had a knack for bringing people together and helping them grow. And I loved the work I was doing.

I started working at the team level, first for smaller programs, then bigger programs, and now for the last four or five years I've been operating at the enterprise level.

About five years ago I took the Co-Active Fundamentals training with Coaches Training Institute (CTI), and the things I learned about myself blew my mind. Yes, I had been doing coaching, but this was taking this coaching to the next level. Something really cleared for me at that time. It felt like a fog lifted for me, and I knew it, this is what I'm set to do; this is what I really wanted to do."

Raquel Silva from London, UK

Raquel was the first internal coach to respond to my request for an interview. She impressed upon me the importance of staying neutral as the internal coach, and that this must be an intentional effort on the part of the coach. She would go on to state that it's far too easy to get absorbed by the internal politics and the culture.

How did Raquel get started in internal coaching?

"When I became an internal coach the main drive was that I'm like a gardener. I like to plant little seeds and see them grow into beautiful plants and flowers. Most of my mentors were internal coaches, and I saw in them the joy of seeing the fruits of their hard work. Becoming a coach myself, during my learning journey, the feeling grows even more.

I work mainly with IT teams, with people who were not feeling empowered to make decisions and stand by their good experience and knowledge. Standing by their side during the journey and being able to support them further is what inspires me to continue as an internal coach."

Richard Lister from London, UK

I was impressed by the lens through which Richard viewed coaching; it was the lens of the storyteller. He recounted several stories of leaders that he had coached, and the subsequent results. I believe that much of Richard's success as an internal coach stems from how he also uses storytelling to communicate with decision-makers about the value of coaching. He also has a knack of taking the hard data that he collects on his clients and converting that data into a story. It is quite impressive.

How did Richard get started in internal coaching?

"I took on a daunting leadership challenge in 2004. How could I lead eighteen direct reports based all across East and Central Africa? It would be impossible to hands-on manage so many people. But it was possible to coach them towards their own wise solutions.

The next phase for me was developing my coaching skills. I learned much of the art of simple but powerful coaching from Claire Pedrick. This led to Tearfund asking me to become an internal coach and to accreditation with the International Coaching Federation.

That's just the mechanics of my journey. The heart is joy. The joy of helping people from feeling burdened to encouraged and from feeling confused to clear. That's why I'm an internal coach."

Syed Ali from Miami, Florida, USA

In my interview with Syed, he focused on an area not addressed by the others: the unique relationship that internal coaches have with other internal coaches within the same organization. He cited the importance of working together as a team of coaches for the betterment of the larger organization.

How did Syed get started in internal coaching?

"My journey as a formal internal agile coach started at Florida Power & Light where, due to my passion, I joined the enterprise coaching team as a part of their graduation program "Coach in Training" when they were hiring internal employees to work with them.

This was a pivotal point for me to learn and evaluate myself about agile coaching. This was a two-year program, where I was mentored and coached by other senior coaches. I was given the opportunity to get further training to polish my facilitation and coaching skills. The best thing was that I was working with agile teams to practice these coaching, facilitation, and training techniques."

Vernon Stinebaker from Hangzhou City, Zhejiang, China

On my next trip to China I plan to have coffee (or tea) with Vernon. He's one of those rare individuals who instantly connect with you and convey an interest in you. In addition, as you will read, Vernon offers keen insight into the distinction between internal and external coaching, as well as coaching and culture.

How did Vernon get started in internal coaching?

"I considered becoming an internal coach in two phases: the first, starting when I first became a team leader/manager, and later as I was exposed to professional coaching. I was never comfortable with a 'command and control' style of management or leadership, so as soon as I became a team leader I worked from a coaching mindset—trust my team, provide them with the support they needed, then get out of their way.

Second, as I was exposed to professional coaching through the Scrum Alliance, individuals with skills beyond my own—Roger Brown, Andrea Tomasini, and John Miller—inspired me to consolidate and formalize my coaching so I became a PCC. I worked within my organization to hand off management responsibility to a colleague so I could focus on coaching more intensively without the encumbrances of having direct reports."

Viktur Glinka from Russia

My ancestral roots include Russia, which piqued my interest when Viktur agreed to an interview for this book. I was pleasantly surprised to learn that coaching is underway in Russia, albeit in the beginning stages. Viktur is one of those early coaches blazing the trail.

I appreciated Viktur's energy and enthusiasm for coaching, especially internal coaching. Clearly having benefited from being coached himself, Viktur is eager to learn more. He also possesses a strong desire to share with others what he has discovered.

How did Viktur get started in internal coaching?

"It's simple. Another internal coach bit me like in a zombie movie. But unlike turning an absent-minded zombie, I got insight into how to bring awareness to my life while achieving goals.

My career started with a project management position. Soon it became clear to me that the traditional project approach makes no sense. I tried plenty of things and finally discovered agile.

According to an agile leader's model of competences, being a coach is its key element. I was wondering what exactly the coach does. Luckily one of my coworkers was the internal coach. She opened up a coaching world for me. Since that I'm really into coaching and helping my colleagues reach their potential."

3 | The guiding principles of coaching

As a backdrop for the guiding principles of internal coaching, I would like to offer the distinction between competencies and guiding principles. To put it succinctly, it is skills versus strategies. Competencies are specific skills or benchmarks that enable one to perform well. For example, in coaching, one of our competencies is active listening. Effective coaching is characterized by active listening.

Guiding principles are approaches, strategies, and perspectives that contribute to the effective use of a competency. For example, one of the guiding principles of coaching is that questions are more important than answers. This guiding principle determines how the coach responds after listening. In this case, rather than providing a client with an answer or solution, the coach asks a question so that the client discovers their own answer.

The guiding principles of coaching below are helpful to both internal and external coaches. The chapters that follow will explore specific guiding principles for internal coaches.

Guiding principles of coaching: a brief overview

1. Create the coaching agreement together. Like a crucible, a coaching agreement provides the safe container for the fire to be focused and used in beneficial ways. Without the crucible, the fire can burn out, or worse yet, burn out of control. Take time to set, and also reset, the coaching agreement with those you coach, both in the short term and long term. The coaches I interviewed had much to say about the coaching agreement. Pradeepa Narayanaswamy reminds us that coaching agreements are not a one-time thing, set in stone. We need to frequently revisit our agreements. She also offered the suggestion of slowing things down at the start of coaching in order to establish the coaching agreement. By slowing things down at the start, the likelihood of buy-in is much greater and in the long run it will speed things up. Cherie Silas spoke of the uniqueness agreements of the internal coach, especially triangle agreements between coach, client, and sponsor. Erkan Kadir added that there are numerous conflicts of interest as an internal coach, which further emphasizes the importance of creating the coaching agreement.

2. Thinking matters. While many begin their coaching by asking their client, "What do you want to talk about today?", I believe that it's much more beneficial to ask, "What do you want to think about today?" Our thinking directly determines what we see as possible, which is directly connected with the action that we take. One of our primary roles as coach is to expand awareness. Expand your client's awareness and you open a whole other world of possibilities. Bring to the surface your client's beliefs and assumptions and often they will see that what once served them well no longer serves them—in fact, it limits them. Elise Shapiro shared that the focus of her coaching is helping organizations and teams move into a modern way of working, which is iterative and customer-centric—facilitating this from a coaching stance.

3. When in doubt simply say, "Say more." Most people find it hard to identify the last time someone listened to them, let alone listened deeply. As part of our listening process, inserting these two words, "Say more," into the conversation invites our clients to share things that have often been unshared and perhaps even unknown by our client. "Say more" also takes the pressure off of the coach when the coach doesn't know what to say.

4. Let silence do the heavy lifting. This is a classic principle that most coaches learn early on. Silence, which many find uncomfortable, has a valuable role in the coaching conversation. Similar to "say more," silence nudges the person to keep talking. Often, what comes out of the silence is something not yet spoken. Vernon Stinebaker spoke with me about the importance of giving your clients white space—silence.

5. The presenting issue is rarely the real issue. Coaches that have previously worked in other helping professions will recognize this principle. Many of our clients either don't know what the real issue is and therefore need to talk their way to the real issue, or they aren't yet certain that the coach is safe enough to share deeply with. Give your clients time to get to the real issue. Alex Sloley commented, "the coach needs to go deeper and even ask, why do you want to change?" His experience has been that there are times when the coaching is a cover for something else.

6. Coach the person, not the problem. Coaching is not solution-focused, rather it is person-focused. While most clients bring a problem or a challenge to the coaching conversation, and while the majority of the coaching time may be spent addressing that problem, the *focus* of the coaching is on developing the individual. By intentionally coaching the person, the next time a similar problem or challenge presents itself, the individual will be better equipped to respond. Kathy Sauve summarized this guiding principle nicely when she said, "Better people equals better leaders."

7. Notice without naming. Our job as coach is to help our clients see, not to see for them. For example, let's say I am coaching someone who is being very animated and excited who suddenly becomes sullen or quiet.

Instead of naming what I think happened, which will often be inaccurate, I can instead ask the client what just happened. The person who makes the discovery owns the discovery. Pradeepa explained that simply being a mirror for our clients can be most beneficial. We can let the client interpret and consider what the mirror is showing them. That's not our job.

8. Listen to the story without getting hooked on it. It is incredibly important that the coach really understands their client. So, we listen carefully and pay close attention to their story. It is equally important, though, that we stay outside the story. Our clients need us to speak truth to them about their situations. Our value, as coaches, is that we offer an outside, unbiased, yet 100% supportive perspective to our clients. Raquel Silva addressed this by advocating that the coach stay neutral—or at least as neutral as possible, since you are part of the system.

9. Excavate the unspoken. We listen not only with our ears, but also with our eyes, intuition, and bodies. Simply put, we need to pay attention and respond to everything we sense, because our clients are often speaking without words. During my interview with Christine Thompson, she said that observation and listening were the keys to coaching. These keys inform the client and coach on the areas that need coaching and enable the coach to "push on the doors," and can also be a mirror reflecting back to the client and larger organization what really is. Viktor Glinka adds, "During the coach session, I carefully watch internal contradictions and try to gauge what is unsaid."

10. Questions are more important than answers. Questions get the client thinking, considering, and wondering, whereas answers stop the process. Once our client is thinking, we can invite them to consider other ways of viewing the same thing. Brain study data tells us that if we are told something, there is very little brain activity involved. When we are asked a question and begin to think about our answer, the brain activity is much more pronounced and the thoughts are better retained.

11. Be curious. From a place of curiosity we are more likely to challenge assumptions, and question the spoken and unspoken rules governing our decisions. When we are curious we tend to naturally pay attention and notice things.

12. Acknowledge. Starting early in childhood, the majority of our thoughts about ourselves are negative, and coaching emerged partly as a response to this epidemic. Coaches purposely choose to affirm the greatness and giftedness of the individual and team. Our belief is that people live into the views that we hold of them. Benjamin Zander's approach is to give people an "A" at the start, and he finds that makes them more likely to achieve that level of success. Allison Pollard enjoys catching her clients in the act of doing something great: "You see some amazing impact. You actually get to witness some of their results and see things happening."

13. Show up slightly under-prepared. Yes, I know this principle seems odd, until you consider that the coaching conversation is organic in nature. If we are too prepared, it's possible that we will miss the moment by not being fully present. By showing up fully present and fully in the moment, we create a space for the conversation to emerge. Of course we still need to do our due diligence, and just be *slightly* under-prepared.

14. The real coaching happens after the coaching. It is not the 30–45-minute coaching session, but rather the time after the session that is most important. It is after the session when the client lives into the insights and decisions of the session; this is when the valuable a-ha's and hmm's are translated into action, behavior, and implementation.

15. Don't pick up where you left off. This guiding principle is closely tied to the previous one, that the real coaching happens after the coaching. Consider that if you pick up where the client was at your last session, in effect you, as the coach, are negating the important after-the-coaching work. Instead, ask for a brief check-in and then ask the focus of today's session. *Get out of the way while also being in the way.* Stay in your role as coach. Hold your nerve when clients are pushing responsibility back to you. Tolerate not knowing. Yet, at the same time, be conscious that you have the potential of slowing them down or disrupting them. When they are on a roll, let them continue.

Guiding principles of internal coaching

We can view coaching as a pendulum swinging from one side to the other. At one end of the pendulum swing would be external coaching, at the other end, internal coaching. End-to-end and what is in between is all coaching. The balance of this book will focus almost exclusively on the internal coaching end of the pendulum.

Before we get into the guiding principles of internal coaching, let's understand this underlying basic truth:

Internal coaching is a hybrid of coaching and whatever else is needed.

As an external coach of twenty years, I have spent the vast majority of my time and energy offering pure coaching, what is sometimes referred to as content-free coaching. While there are times when I have stepped out of the role of coach into another profession, role, or discipline, internal coaches step in and out of their roles all the time. Many of the internal coaches that I interviewed referred to this as switching hats.

Routinely, internal coaches begin with the coaching mindset or stance and then switch hats based on what will be most helpful for the client. Based on my interviews, it appears that internal coaching is a true hybrid—fully coaching and fully whatever else is needed. Most often that appeared to be a blend of coaching and consulting—or coach-sulting.

During my formative years as a coach, I was introduced to the distinction between content-free coaching versus content-rich coaching. Content-free coaching tends to be what many refer to as pure coaching—the one-hat coach. And at the other end of the continuum is content-rich coaching, which weaves into the coaching conversation the rich expertise of the coach—multiple-hat coaching. When done well, the multiple-hat approach aligns nicely with the expert-to-expert coaching mindset described earlier, and explored in depth in the following chapter.

The multiple-hat coaching approach seems to be a practical outcome of living (coaching) in your mess, a term coined by Vernon Stinebaker and discussed in depth in a later chapter. As an external coach, you interact with your clients on a twice-monthly basis—or at best a weekly basis. Lots of ground is covered by your client in between sessions as they use the skills and resources available to them to meet their daily challenges.

The internal coach, on the other hand, is living in the mess of that daily life, right alongside their clients. The successful internal coach needs to have a toolbox filled with resources, skills, and expertise right at their fingertips, which they can pull out at a moment's notice.

Elise Shapiro noted that internal coaches need to learn how to mix different coaching tools and frameworks together to do the best thing for their clients. It's one thing to know a coaching framework or a model and to use that exclusively. It is quite another skill to seamlessly integrate all types of tools into your coaching.

Richard Lister estimated that his time is typically spent in an 80:20 split, with about 80% coaching and 20% mentoring. Much of Elise's coaching is a blended role, with 30–40% being pure coaching and the majority being a mix of disciplines and modalities.

The chapters that follow will explore the following guiding principles specifically for internal coaches. Some of these will be similar to the guiding principles above, with various adaptations and emphasis. Others are unique for internal coaches.

The guiding principles of internal coaching are:

1 The coaching stance
2 Expert-to-expert
3 Contracting matters
4 Agents of awareness
5 Coaching initiative
6 Coach the system
7 Live with your mess
8 Confidentiality, yes. Secret-keeping, no!
9 Who coaches the coach?
10 Demonstrate your worth
11 Give conflict a voice

4 | Guiding principle #1: The coaching stance— it always begins with listening

While there are numerous unique features to internal coaching, there is at least one commonality between internal and external coaching. This commonality is the starting point of all coaching. We refer to this starting point as the coaching mindset or, in some instances, the coaching stance. Regardless of the topic or focus of the coaching conversation, the coaching stance is the same:

Coaching always begins with listening.

Coach Vernon Stinebaker uses a story about the renowned artist Michelangelo to highlight the coaching mindset. Someone once asked Michelangelo how he was able to create his lovely statue of David and he replied, "David was always in there. I just chipped away the rock that was covering this inner angel." Similarly, the coach is listening for the inner David in each client they coach. Our starting point is that everything our client needs is in them, we just need to help them chip things away to reveal their inner angel. Coaching begins with listening so that the client and coach can become aware of and draw out the inner angel.

While there are many professionals that are trained to listen to their client, the listening of the coach is different and distinct.

Coaches listen from curiosity

Coaches listen from a place of curiosity. We listen from a place of not knowing, whereas most other professionals listen from a place of knowing, or expertise. Coaches not only begin with not knowing, we are also very comfortable with not knowing. In fact, even if we have successfully coached many people on the same topic of our client and even if we have a pretty good idea of what steps our client needs to take, we initially set that knowledge off to the side. Why do we do this? Because we believe that our clients have the answer within them and that it is much more effective if our client makes their own discovery, as opposed to the coach telling them what to do.

On a personal note, this "not knowing" of the coach has sparked a humorous response from my mom. When her friends ask her what I'm doing, she responds,

"Val is a coach." Her friends follow up with, "What's a coach?" My mother responds, "I'm not quite sure. All I know is that people call him on the phone, he doesn't tell them what to do, and they pay him."

Coaches listen longer

A second characteristic of how coaches listen is that the coach listens *longer* than most other professionals. Consider this: on average, patients get about 11 seconds to explain the reasons for their visit before they are interrupted by their doctors (Singh Ospina et al. 2019). These authors go on to state that when the doctor does interrupt, it is not to ask for additional helpful information, rather it is to begin to offer their diagnosis.

Coaches are trained to listen longer. In fact, most coaches spend 80–90% of their time listening. One of the reasons that the coach listens longer is that, as stated in the previous paragraphs, since we do not know and believe that our client does know, we want and need to hear from our client.

On many occasions, I have observed that all my client really needed was someone to listen to them—period! The simple act of getting their thoughts out of their head and hearing them out loud was catalytic. When the coach does speak, it's usually in the form of a question. We believe that questions are more important than answers and that questions help reveal the "inner David."

Coaches listen for possibility

A third characteristic of the coach's listening is that we listen for possibility. We pay particular attention to what is emerging, or wanting to emerge. We are not listening to fix anything.

Several years ago, I was facilitating a coach training for a large group of federal prison chaplains. Partway through the training one of the chaplains interrupted me and stated, "Why are we learning how to coach? We work with inmates that are obviously broken and need fixing."

Before I could answer, another chaplain responded saying, "Yes, clearly our clients are broken and in need of fixing. And they also need hope. As a chaplain, I might be the first to see something good in an inmate." Martin Seligman (1998) said that treatment is "not about fixing what's broken; it is nurturing what is best within ourselves."

Coaches listen to expand awareness

A fourth characteristic of the coach's listening is that the coach listens to identify and expand the awareness and perceptions of the client—not because they are wrong, rather to discover the lens through which the client is viewing the world. Similar to a routine eye exam in which various lenses are substituted for better vision, the coaching process seeks to develop the individual or team by expanding their awareness.

Let me offer a humorous personal example of expanding awareness. I grew up with a world map which had the Atlantic Ocean in the center with the United States/North America prominent on one side and Europe on the other side. I was taught that this is what the world looks like. Several years ago while in Seoul, South Korea, I saw a map of the world displayed on a wall. I literally stopped in my tracks and thought to myself, "That's not right!"

You see, in this map, South Korea and Asia were in the center and most prominent. And then it struck me. This was the same world from a different perspective.

A short time after this experience I was recounting this story to friends of mine in Sao Paulo, Brazil. The next day, to my surprise, they presented me with a map of the world saying, "This is how the world really is." This map had South America on top, with North America below. It was upside-down ... or was it? A Talmudic concept came to my mind at that moment: "We do not see things as they are. We see things as we are."

Much of the work of the coach is simply helping people to see the same thing differently. Another concept that resonates with this topic of greater awareness is that there is more than one right answer. We all have developed patterns of thought and behavior that may have served us well at one point, yet now they are limiting what is possible.

Listening in internal coaching

In our interview, Pauline Gallien shared a recurring experience of listening as an internal coach. "A person comes to me. They are looking for answers. Instead, I ask coaching questions. The person leaves, thanking me for my 'advice' when I gave no advice, just coached."

Brock Argue recounts that a conversation between the internal coach and manager commonly starts, "I'm having trouble with my team. Go fix them." Instead of moving right into fix-it mode, Brock begins with the coaching mindset and asks questions: Why do you think there's a problem with the team? What do you think I can do about it? After listening to the team members, he goes back to the team leader with, "Okay, based on what I've discovered, here's what I think I can do."

When asked to describe a typical day in the life of an internal coach, Elise Shapiro responded by saying that while she wasn't sure that there was such a thing as a typical day, one thing that was typical though was that every encounter of an internal coach begins with the coaching mindset. She also reported that much of the coach's work is simply mirroring back to the organization what we have observed, and the shared themes or patterns of what the individuals have been telling us.

Richard Lister offers this example of a coach's listening:

"I had a fantastic experience in South Asia, coaching a guy as we bumped along in a four-wheel-drive pickup truck, heading off to see a site. I was just talking to him about his vision, and helping him to clarify the scale of his vision. His vision was for the entire country. And I was able to help him to crystallize that, and think about his key steps for planning that into reality.

I had a very encouraging conversation with him four years later, which was just a few months ago. And he said, 'That vision, that conversation, remains with me.' I only spent three or four days with him, but that one particular conversation crystallized an amazing amount."

Mauricio Robles shared that the combination of observation and listening proved to be invaluable as a coach, and that as coaches we need to take the time to observe and listen before we even begin working with our clients. We need to observe how they are interacting with each other and notice their language—both spoken and body language. It's equally important to listen to what is not being said. For example, who is looking at whom during the group interactions. Or, who seems to be withholding information from the larger group.

Taking a coaching stance with a new manager

Pradeepa Narayanaswamy offers an example of how taking a coaching stance positively impacted the behavior of a manager she coached:

"I was partnering with the senior director of an organization, who was a very good leader, and they asked me to work with a new manager to help them grow their leadership skills.

This new manager had come from a very technical background and had never managed people before. They were always an independent contributor to their team, and they were excellent, very brilliant in what they had to bring to the table.

Because of their brilliance and what they had contributed to their company, that organization promoted this person to be the manager. And now they were responsible for a whole lot of people. So they were really struggling, because they had no training in how to manage people. They were always used to being in the spotlight themselves, and now were asking, 'How can I grow a bunch of people and bring them into the spotlight? Now what will happen to my spotlight,' right? So there was that dilemma and that contradiction.

This person had never had a good experience working with other coaches and other people in that space. I was new to this organization, and right off the bat this person just doesn't like me. Because I'm coming in as a coach they have this preconceived notion that I'm 'one of them.' I'm going to come and tell them what's wrong with them and have them change. So there's already this block.

So there was this pushback, but we started having conversations. We started creating our agreement, how you and I are going to work together, what can you expect from me, and what can I expect from you, and how is this mutually agreeable to us?

So we were trying to co-create that agreement between us, and this person never expected that in our first conversation. They were all aloof and like, 'Okay Pradeepa, tell me what I should be doing. What am I doing wrong? Tell me what I should be fixing.' They were pretty sour about it.

So I say, 'Okay, let's take a step back. I have zero idea how to answer that question, but let's figure out how this is going to go, how we are going to enter into a professional relationship with this, and if this is something that we want to continue, let's put it on paper as to how you and I are going to work together.' I sure don't think they expected all that, right?

So I kept my stance on that. It was quite helpful for them to understand the power of creating an agreement, of mutually co-creating an agreement. And I was challenging them. Instead of giving them the answer to the questions, I was challenging them to take a different perspective. I was helping them explore it using a question. I gave them homework of, 'Okay, why don't you think about this and maybe in our next conversation, we can explore that a little further.'

So it was a work in progress, initially. But then they were starting to apply that approach they were learning with their team, and they started seeing results in actually becoming a different leader. This did not happen in one day, but over the course of time they started seeing how their team was respecting them, coming to them and asking for help as a manager, not fearing them as a manager. And the relationship seemed to become more open and transparent and started to become fun.

They realized that they were changing. They weren't changing the team, but they were changing in how they were showing up as a new manager for the team, and the team was welcoming that.

They were taking a different stance as a manager, and how they wanted to show up, and this started showing up in how the team was perceiving this manager. And nevertheless to say, they started liking this new person as their boss.

And this organization has a quarterly anonymous survey that goes out to the team, where they have to rate their managers. And guess what? This person's score drastically improved from their previous rating. And this person who started out hating me and my presence, became my biggest advocate, pushing his peers to work with me and to get coaching.

So I'll always remember this person, because it was somebody who was forced into coaching by their boss. They never wanted it. They hated the idea, and they had this preconception of what I was going to tell them or teach them. But then they realized that's not what true coaching is."

Some questions that an internal coach can ask themselves to be sure that they are approaching their client from a coaching stance include:

- What can I do to radically increase my focus on my client's inner David?
- On a scale of 1 to 10 (1 = no curiosity, 10 = extremely curious), how curious am I about what my client wants coaching on?
- What additional things do I need to hear from my client?
- What is driving my listening? A fixer mindset? Curiosity? My own brilliance?
- What is the primary lens that my client is looking through? What other lenses might they substitute?
- What are my beliefs about my client and the situation they are bringing to me, and their capability to address this?

Additional questions to consider:

- If listening longer became a norm across your organization, what impact would this have on your organization's current goals and objectives?
- What is one simple step you can take to develop greater listening within your organization? (Remember, this question is about what step YOU can take, not ANYONE ELSE.)
- How can listening be rewarded?

5 Guiding principle #2: Expert-to-expert—hat switching

This guiding principle speaks to the unique relationship between the coach and client, which in a nutshell is: expert-to-expert. The coach relates to their client believing that the person that they are about to coach is basically healthy and whole. They are the experts of their own lives and have within themselves the ability and capability to move forward in healthy, constructive ways, both professionally and personally.

This starting point is different from the typical professional relationship in which the professional is viewed as the expert having all the answers for their client, the non-expert. The expert-to-non-expert relationship does not see the person as basically healthy and whole and therefore focuses on what needs to be fixed and what is broken.

In the expert-to-expert relationship, we acknowledge that the coach has expertise as a result of their coach training, expertise and life experiences. In this relationship though, the coach intentionally holds back on their expertise, choosing to share it only when it empowers and benefits the client. At this point they would acknowledge that they are switching "hats" or roles.

The expert-to-expert relationship is much more pronounced in the internal coaching relationship than in the external coaching relationship. During a typical internal coaching conversation, the internal coach switches hats not only sooner than the typical external coach, but much more frequently. Part of the reason for this distinction is that the internal coach is providing on-the-spot coaching on a daily basis (see Guiding principle #7: Live with your mess), as well as other expertise as needed by their client.

The seasoned internal coach always begins with the expertise of their client and, going forward, is able to seamlessly switch hats mid-conversation, giving their client just enough of their expertise to keep them moving forward. Viktor Glinka shares that internal coaches wear many different hats, and regardless of which hat you are wearing or which role you are in, you start with the coaching mindset (and relationship). So, if you're a facilitator, you start by coaching and then you move into facilitating. If you're a consultant, you start as a coach and then you start telling.

Learning how to listen first, and tell later

A common misnomer that I hear from many new coaches is the idea that coaches never give their clients advice or share their expertise. This is false. What is true is that we begin by intentionally holding back our advice and expertise, resisting the urge to make assumptions about our clients and their situation. Instead, we begin by really listening. We want to listen to all that they have to say and share about their scenario.

As we proceed, we believe that, for the most part, our clients have within them what they need to continue, or it is near the surface and needs further development. We also recognize that our clients are also human beings, and from time to time, will also need outside resources and expertise. Sometimes the most empowering thing that a coach can do is to offer advice or share their expertise and then jump back into the role of coach.

My favorite way of explaining this misnomer to new coaches is the following:

I am right-handed. I would like to be ambidextrous. Step 1 of this process is to use my left hand instead of my right hand. An easy way to do this is to put my right hand behind my back so that I am not tempted to use it. If I do this enough, eventually my left hand develops greater skill and technique. But this is only Step 1, because my goal is not to become left-handed, rather it is to become ambidextrous. So, Step 2 is to no longer keep my right hand behind my back, rather to bring my right hand to the front so that I am free to use whichever hand I want.

It's the same with learning how to coach. The first step for most new coaches is to stop telling people what to do. Primarily because the ways that we tell and offer advice aren't helpful. So, we stop telling and start listening and asking questions. Then, once we've become competent at listening and asking powerful questions, we bring our advice and expertise back into the picture. Because our goal is to be masterful with all of the tools that we have available, including advice-giving.

We've already discussed that what differentiates the internal coach from the external coach is that the internal coach switches hats not only sooner than the typical external coach, but much more frequently. Cherie Silas elaborates further by adding that, "Your role as an internal coach is not just coach. You're coaching, you're facilitating, you're sometimes doing training. And then there is the agile piece, when you're doing consulting and actually giving your personal opinion. You're doing all of this from a coaching stance."

Elise Shapiro said that on any given day she ends up wearing a lot of different hats, always beginning from the coaching stance. "It's very much a blended role. I might do pure coaching about 30–40% of my time, and then it's mixed with other disciplines and modalities."

The challenges of hat switching

Claire Bamberg highlighted one challenge when we warn internal coaches of being very careful not to do your clients' work for them. We need to be clear in our agreements with our clients regarding what is their work and their responsibility, and what is ours.

Madhavi Ledalla addresses another challenge as a very real temptation when starting internal coaching with an organization. "The organization has high hopes for us [internal coaches]. We tend to get into the consulting mode because we want to give solutions and we want to ensure that we can show results quickly." She asserts, "Stay in true coach mode." Switch hats only when needed or called for.

Christine Thompson highlighted another challenge when she raised the question of timing. Is this the right time for coaching, or is something else needed? Christine's comment reminds us of one of the guiding principles that underlies all coaching, whether external or internal (see Chapter 3), which is:

Get out of the way while also being in the way.

Stay in your role as coach. Hold your nerve when clients are pushing responsibility back to you. Tolerate not knowing. Yet, at the same time, be conscious that you have the potential of slowing them down or disrupting them. When they are on a roll, let them continue.

Some questions that an internal coach can ask themselves to be sure that they are fostering an expert-to-expert relationship include:

- Whose expertise is driving the coaching conversation?
- What's great about my client? Name three things.
- What would a coaching conversation with my client look like if I gave them an "A"?
- What are the signs and signals that my client needs me to offer them advice?
- Which hat (role) does my client need from me right now?
- Who is working hardest in this coaching session, my client or me?

Additional questions to consider:

- If your current leadership adopted a "listen more, tell less" approach, what would you have more of? Less of?
- What additional support can you offer those who regularly switch hats?
- This section addresses the need to unlearn how to give advice. What else needs to be unlearned in your organization?

6 | Guiding principle #3: Contracting matters— agreements and relationships

As an external coach serving individual or corporate clients, there are typically one or two parties in each coaching relationship. There is your client, which may be an individual, a team, or a group. Then there might also be a payee or sponsor—the one who brought you in to coach that person or group. That makes external coaching a *one-to-one* or a *one-to-two* model.

As an internal coach working within an organization, however, you need to manage multiple relationships. It's a *one-to-many* model.

One of the first relationships you have as an internal coach is with the sponsor—whoever is bringing you into the role—typically a supervisor, manager, or department head. This is who supervises you and coordinates your work, and this is who advocates for funding for the coaching—the payee or sponsor, just like in external coaching.

Then there are your clients, and there are lots of them: teams, groups, and individuals. And you will need to have agreements and relationships with all of them, so you can be clear about what you can expect from them, and what they can expect from you.

Brock Argue suggests the coaching agreement include things like:

- Being clear on what everyone is doing
- The length of the coaching engagement
- What you will do as the coach, as well as what you won't be doing
- How you will measure success
- Checkpoints
- How, when, and to whom feedback will be given.

Another thing to contract from the very beginning is buy-in and support, right from the top. Otherwise, as Pradeepa Narayanaswamy warns, you'll face an uphill battle with management that doesn't understand what coaching is.

"My boss did a wonderful job creating an agreement with the organization's senior VP that I was supporting on how this relationship is going to work. And because she did that so beautifully, he actually listed me, my name, as a direct report in his organization chart. There was his name, and then in the box next to his, it said Pradeepa, coach. He wanted to show his entire organization that he was taking my role seriously and he was giving me all the support that I want, that he was behind me and would back me up. That was really, really critical."

Conflict can happen

But what about when your agreement with one client or set of clients overlaps with your agreement with another? This convergence of client agreements (sometimes known as conflicts of interest) becomes another type of relationship.

For example, a supervisor having a coaching session may mention the name of an employee. Meanwhile, the internal coach may also be coaching the individual mentioned in the session, even if they're in another department. Sometimes the convergence is more subtle, where even the possibility of conflict can create issues. One internal coach shared that they must be careful about even being seen talking to a supervisor because people could read something into that.

Erkan Kadir shared these thoughts about potential conflicts of interest:

"As an internal coach you're not really neutral when you're part of the organization because you have opinions on things. And you might have conflicts of interest because your boss has certain goals and they collide with the individual you are coaching.

Know what those conflicts of interest are and then be explicit about them with the people you're working with in your coaching agreement and just design around them. For example, say: 'Hey, look I just spent a year coaching this person that you're having problems with.' There are all types of soap opera type situations."

Cherie Silas also reminds coaches to watch for triangle agreements between the coach, client, and sponsor/supervisor. These need to be discussed and agreed upon before any coaching begins.

Allison Pollard says that it is extremely important that the internal coach navigate the relationships and agreements well. Pradeepa encourages the coach to go slow to go fast, meaning that you take extra time to be really clear about the agreement and relationship and that by going slower at the start you will actually cover more ground in the long run. She also reminds internal coaches to revisit their agreements often. Agreements are not a one-time deal, set in stone.

Coaching the system

There is a third relationship in internal coaching. The third relationship is with the system, which you've likely been brought in to change. So, you are in essence coaching the system. Ideally, as you change things in the small unit you are working with, that impact will spread throughout the organization.

Unfortunately, that doesn't often happen because the change is frequently stopped at a higher level of leadership.

There is an interesting twist to the coaching agreement when you are also coaching the system. Remember, as an internal coach you are coaching the system, while you are also part of the system. Allison calls this being in the picture. Madhavi Ledalla says that as an internal coach you not only have knowledge of how the organization works, but you also get to know the internal culture of the organization.

The internal coach has a large sphere of influence because they can interact with anyone in the organization; they have reachability. So, they get to understand the actual culture because they talk to everyone in the organization and they are part of the game.

Claire Bamberg emphasized that internal coaches need to be aware that they are working within a system and the system contains their work. An internal coach is part of that system and must pay attention to all those dynamics. As an external coach, on the other hand, you entrust the client with their ability to sort that through.

Cherie says that when coaching the system, the internal coach needs to remember that they have a stake in the game. You, as an employee, are part of the system. "Be careful not to push your agenda. You have to always seek neutrality and neutral space. You need to keep holding the client as a client, not a co-worker. Keep the mindset of they are a client. My boss is my client. My co-workers are my clients, my client is a client." Christine Thompson's way of remembering this when walking into the building is to pause briefly, to remember to leave herself at the door.

It's important for internal coaches to recognize the multidimensional, multi-faceted nature of these three coaching relationships, and how different this is from external coaching. This applies in corporate coaching, business coaching, as well as in non-profit settings.

Some questions that an internal coach can ask themselves to be sure that they have established a solid coaching agreement include:

- What is my responsibility? What is my client's responsibility?
- What are the parties involved in this coaching agreement? Client, sponsor, manager, etc.
- How will we know that we are being successful?
- What are the signs and signals of possible conflicts of interest?
- Who can help me identify possible conflicts of interest?

Additional questions to consider:

- In additional to the coaches on your team, who else within your organization is involved in *one-to-many* relationships?
- Name three potential conflicts of interest within your organization that need to be addressed, right here, right now!
- Who can help address these potential conflicts of interest?

7 Guiding principle #4: Agents of awareness

The name of this guiding principle was inspired by my interview with coach Alex Sloley, who sees the role of internal coach as an agent of awareness versus an agent of change. This is an important distinction for the coach, as well as the organization, to understand. Many organizations hire internal coaches because they have identified an area or issue that needs to change, and they bring in an expert to facilitate that change.

Yet while change happens in coaching, change is more accurately defined as the outcome of the greater awareness that comes from the coaching conversation. "As the agent of awareness," Alex continues, "you're helping everybody around you become aware of what's going on, and then helping them learn how to change it themselves." As coaches, he says, "When you go into an organization and they tell you what to change, my biggest warning would be to ask *why they want the change*."

Coaches have different ways of describing this practice and concept of increasing awareness. Pradeepa Narayanaswamy sees her role as showing the leaders and teams a mirror, so that they can see for themselves.

Christine Thompson employs a process called shadow coaching, specifically looking for patterns that help articulate the unique DNA or system at play within the organization, which she then mirrors back to the organization and its leaders.

Mauricio Robles reminds the new coach of the value of observing and listening, especially at the start of a coaching engagement. "One of the things that has proven to be very valuable to me is to take the time to observe and listen to [the] team you are coaching before starting to work with them. Look at the way they [are] interacting with each other—the language, the inflections of the voice, the information being shared."

Kathy Sauve sees the coach as the bridge between what operational leaders are feeling and what senior leaders are aspiring to do. "I'm not an advocate for people. I don't see myself as the advocate for everybody and I can fix it all. I think I'm a bridge to make sure that people are hearing each other. A bridge does not have feelings one way or another. Its goal is to bring the two together."

She recounts the following example:

"I had a manager I had to let go, and then there was a lot of fallout from the stuff that happens after a manager leaves. And I was watching this one person I think was struggling because of that. I went through my really good questions, and then said to her, 'I would love to just go and have a chat with you.'

She and I went to a room, and I just said, 'You've been a good performer in the past. I see you're struggling with what's happening.' So I went totally coach-like with it and listened to her and realized some of the things we were trying to fix were actually making it worse because I didn't know she had a mental health issue.

This is something she hadn't shared with anyone outside her family. The conversation became very collaborative. I took a very coach-like stance with her by trying to understand, asking her for input on what she thought that she could do. How could we support her? What did she need? Not that it didn't have bumps, but you could just see it working.

We were able to get down to, 'How does this issue show up in your work? How can you start to identify it? What would be your first sign?' So asking those good questions for that self-awareness. 'And how can we support you? Who's the best person to support you?' We asked all those questions and she really came up with it and then we just watched this tremendous thing happen.

And then after she got on track, and I had a manager then that walked every step with her to give support. I would do check-ins with her, and I asked her for feedback. 'I decided to be a coach with you, and I want to know how it felt.' She said it was fantastic. She talked about how partnering it was, how collaborative it was. By the end of the year, she was exceeding the expectations of the role."

Madhavi Ledalla begins every coaching engagement with a discovery assessment process. Instead of jumping in right away to solve a problem or implement a change, she first meets with every member of the team or department. She meets with them individually, as well as a whole team. During this phase she is noticing their ways of interacting. She is paying attention to what's being said with words, as well as what's being communicated non-verbally. She also asks each individual a series of questions:

- What is going well in the current way of working?
- What are the pain points that they are trying to overcome?
- What are they actually trying to solve?

Once complete, Madhavi collates everything and presents it back to the leaders and the team in an information-sharing phase, so that they can see the differing perspectives. She reports that sometimes the leaders perceive X, while the team perceives Y. There is a disconnect. "My role as coach is to make this information visible. I help them develop greater awareness."

She concludes the information-sharing phase with a handful of questions. "Now that you have a clear picture of your current state," she asks:

- "What do you want to do? And, why?
- What is it that you really want to solve?

- What is your vision?
- What is the transformation road map?
- How do you want to start?"

Awareness requires readiness

The responsibility of awareness doesn't entirely fall on the coach. There also needs to be a readiness to entertain and consider new ways. As agents of awareness we want to be looking for readiness in our clients. Consider the following experience I had coaching an organization recently:

A large organization invited me to participate in their monthly staff training day. I was brought in to teach them coaching skills, but here's what I noticed. When I put people into groups to practice coaching, the energy in the room just skyrocketed—I could hardly bring them back.

Over lunchtime, I wondered if maybe what this group really wanted and needed was group coaching. I mentioned this to one of my hosts and she jumped in with full agreement, so that's how we spent our afternoon.

Now, I'm not suggesting that every time you're contracted to do one thing you shift and offer another, but this was about recognizing readiness for coaching.

This group was giving off bold capital neon lights of readiness. And I'm glad we had the flexibility to go with that because coaching comes so much easier when clients are ready.

As I look back over my last twenty years as a coach, there have been more times than I'd like to admit when a group or person wasn't ready, and I coached them anyway. This situation is frustrating for the coach, who ends up doing more work than they should. That's the tell. It's exhausting and depleting, instead of energizing and fulfilling.

It's not good for the client either, because personal development requires them to use their own resources. Otherwise, it's like going to the gym and paying someone else to go on the treadmill for you, or taking piano lessons but having someone else sit and practice.

When I look back on calls that I haven't looked forward to as much, it's because that readiness wasn't completely there and that meant I had to muster up more readiness. It doesn't serve either party well because the development doesn't happen, or it starts to happen and stops.

These days I do strive to speak up if I sense someone isn't ready for coaching. I ask what it might look like for them to be ready, and what it might take. I describe how it would sound to me if they were ready. Hearing that distinction can be a powerful catalyst for the client.

So, what does coaching readiness look like? The client will be quick to engage in deep conversation. Or, if the person is an introvert, they might be equally quick to dive into deep thought. It feels like there's a lot to do, and that just comes out. The coach can't engage the client quickly enough. We're not talking about a fast pace necessarily, but an eagerness to get to the next step and the next one after that.

The energy is there, and while they want you as the coach to engage them, they also want you to get out of the way and not manage them. It's kind of like using a hula hoop—once you get it going, it doesn't require a whole lot of motion.

Ready clients are in motion. They're going. They don't require a lot of the coach. They need you to be there, but not managing or over-managing. They want to commit, even though they may not know what they're going to commit to yet. They want to take action.

And that's what I heard in this staff training. They started out by saying what other people needed to do to fix the problems in their workplace. When I asked them to reflect on what actions they were willing to take themselves, after a while they realized they needed to be invested in these solutions. And that investment was there. They were ready.

Some questions that an internal coach can ask themselves to be sure that they are focused on developing greater awareness in their clients include:

- What am I noticing about my client? About myself?
- What is my client's non-verbal communication telling me?
- How invested am I in the outcome?
- Do I see myself more as an advocate or a bridge?
- On a scale of 1 to 10 (1 = not ready, 10 = ready), how ready is my client for new awareness?

Additional questions to consider:

- Identify one current goal or objective within your organization, then answer the following question: *What are you actually trying to solve?*
- How can you help others become more aware of what needs to change and why?
- What is your belief about change within your organization?

8 Guiding principle #5: Coaching initiative

The typical external coaching conversation is one in which the client takes the initiative and schedules (initiates) the coaching conversation. The direction goes from client to coach. It is rare, almost non-existent, for the external coach to contact the client to initiate the coaching conversation.

A distinctive feature of internal coaching is that the coaching initiative is multidirectional. The internal coaching conversation can be initiated from many sources: the client, the supervisor, the sponsor, top-tier leadership, or even the coach. The internal coach, because they are an integral part of the daily work environment, frequently take the initiative to engage in the coaching conversation. This is more than the occasional occurrence, rather it is an essential component of the day-to-day workplace environment of the internal coach.

There are several benefits of this multidirectional coaching initiative. One of the benefits is time savings. There is no wait-and-see delay in scheduling or second-guessing by the client as to whether or not coaching is really needed. Potential clients have easy access to you on a daily basis, and as the coach, you can initiate a conversation with an employee and begin to lay the groundwork for the coaching relationship long before they are ready to begin coaching. This relational groundwork is advantageous when the individual or team is ready to begin coaching. They already know you and hopefully have developed a level of trust.

Erkan Kadir expands on the importance of people getting to know you, as the coach, prior to any coaching engagement. He says, "How you show up matters. They need to see you as successful." In other words, every observation and conversation with the internal coach is either confirming that you are someone that can be of help to them, or not. They are also noticing how you handle confidentiality, conflicts of interest, and difficult conversations.

Another benefit the coaching initiative offers is that you can "catch them in the act." You observe firsthand the interactions and behaviors of teams and individual members. In addition to time savings, already mentioned, you do not need to rely on the anecdotal recounting of events by the client or supervisor.

Allison Pollard says that you see the amazing impact that coaching has on your clients. You actually witness some of their results. You also get to know the context that they are in. You see how they show up on their good days and bad days. And you get to know many of the key players discussed in your coaching conversations. You know your client's supervisor, peers, and other stakeholders. This is beneficial not only at the start of the coaching engagement, but also as the engagement continues and clients take action to improve. Unlike the external coach who hears about successes, challenges, and learning at one- to two-week intervals, the internal coach observes these almost daily. When needed, the coach and clients can have brief laser coaching conversations at any moment.

A final benefit of the coaching initiative is that you are regularly demonstrating your value. Others, especially the decision-makers, see you and your worth firsthand (we'll discuss this much more in Guiding principle #10: Demonstrate your worth).

In our interviews, I shared with both Erkan and Brock Argue that as an external coach, I spend about 30-40% of my time each month focused on marketing—what I refer to as keeping the pipeline filled. My monthly marketing activities include writing, speaking, promptly returning emails and phone calls, keeping relationships warm, and investing in my connectors (people who know people and know how to make things happen).

Internal coaches also have to fill their pipeline

I also offered that prior to writing this book that my assumption had been that internal coaches don't have to worry about keeping their pipeline full. As an employee they have a ready supply of clients to coach.

Erkan and Brock, along with many other internal coaches, confirmed that a common mistake among internal coaches is to not really worry about the pipeline. Many go about their work as an internal coach believing that the company will provide them with the clients to coach. They also assume that the company leadership knows—and will remember—the value that coaching brings to the company.

Nothing could be further from the truth! Internal coaches need to be telling the story of coaching in an ongoing manner, helping others to see the value generated by an internal coach.

Erkan commented that many internal coaches are not well adept at demonstrating the value they provide, and he feels it is absolutely essential that they be able to talk about the value of coaching and take it one step further and quantify their value.

Challenges of coaching initiative

While there are numerous benefits of coaching initiative, there are also a few challenges and concerns. One is that, as the coach, you are always on. You are in coach mode from the moment you enter the building until you leave. This is why Pradeepa Narayanaswamy says that every coach needs a coach, "because we really need to be grounded."

Harris Christopoulos offers the following advice to internal coaches, "Be a continuous learner. Read, and attend training events and conferences. Always be learning something new as a coach to keep yourself fresh."

A second challenge of coaching initiative is resisting the urge to step in too soon. By stepping in too soon you can disempower your client and cut short their growth opportunity. Before exercising your initiative as a coach, ask yourself for whose benefit you are taking this initiative.

A third challenge is that there can be a perceived conflict of interest. For example, you may be coaching an individual and later that same day have a conversation with their immediate supervisor. While you are simply developing a relationship with their supervisor for possible future coaching, your client may think you are talking about them. Here's where creating agreements, demonstrating confidentiality, and embodying integrity will pay off for you and your clients.

Some questions that an internal coach can ask themselves to be sure that they are leveraging their initiative as a coach include:

- What is driving my initiative? My need? My client's need?
- How frequently do I catch my client in the act of doing something great?
- What will I do today (this week) to begin developing relationships with potential clients?
- How will I know if I have stepped in too soon with a client?

Additional questions to consider:

- Are you more likely to "catch someone in the act" of making a mistake or being great?
- What impact would it have on others if you intentionally decided to catch people being great? What impact would it have on you?
- Identify two or three individuals who, if they heard the powerful stories of coaching, could become major advocates of coaching within your organization?

9 Guiding principle #6: Coach the system

As an internal coach there are three possible clients to coach: individuals, teams/groups, and the organization itself. Internal coach Cherie Silas refers to this third entity as coaching at the systemic level. Other internal coaches have referred to this as coaching the DNA or coaching the culture. I am drawing attention to these three possible clients to coach because it is absolutely critical that the internal coach be aware of and coach all three, especially the third entity.

One of the common mistakes that I see new coaches make when coaching teams and groups is that they do a version of "round robin" coaching. They coach one member of the group in front of the others, then move on to the next person to coach. If we were to chart the course of the conversation, it would depict a "hub-and-spoke" system, from coach to individual and back to coach—over and over.

A key to coaching groups and teams is seeing the group or team as a whole—a single unit. Instead of a "hub-and-spoke" type of conversation, it would look more like a "web," the conversation crisscrossing between the various members of the group. I suggest to new coaches that this enables the coach to discover and draw out the who-ness of the group or team.

Systemic coaching takes the "web" conversation to a whole new level. In systemic coaching the focus is on the who-ness of the larger system. When engaged in systemic coaching, the coach is intentionally noticing the patterns, behaviors, and language of the larger culture.

Similar to coaching groups and teams, when coaching the system you want to draw out from the members not only what they are noticing, but also what informs and impacts their noticing. Examples of questions that I ask are:

- What are 10 things that I absolutely need to know about your organization? (I ask each individual to write down their answers, then I collect and collate the answers, and then have the group narrow that large list down to 10.)
- Tell me the "creation story" of this organization, i.e., how and why was it formed?
- How are decisions made in this organization? What are the unspoken/unwritten rules?
- When you first started working here, what did you notice or question that you no longer notice or question?

The key to this line of questioning is the "web" version of conversing. In essence, I want to facilitate a conversation between the members and make sure that all of their voices are heard—not only by me, but more importantly by the leaders of the organization.

When you as an internal coach are new to an organization, I strongly suggest two things with regard to systems:

1   Routinely remind yourself that you are part of the system. The organization that has hired you has a system in place and you are now working within that system.

2   Because you are new to the system, you bring a unique and valuable perspective to the organization. Part of your job is to pay attention to the system. Intentionally notice patterns, behavior, language—especially insider language, behavior, and slang. Later on, once you are fully embedded in the organization, you will be less likely to notice the unique subtleties of the system. Claire Bamberg commented that as an internal coach, "You provide the system a balcony view they might not otherwise have."

Mauricio Robles noted that maybe the greatest risk when working as an internal coach is to normalize the dysfunctionalities of the organization. "I always try to keep myself curious and creative, to keep questioning why this process is done like this. How can the team make it better? Which metric are we missing here? When I hear the infamous 'because that's how we've always done it,' that sets a red light flashing in my head."

What is a system, and how do you coach one?

A system is any group of interdependent people with a shared goal or common interest. An image that Erkan Kadir likes to use for the system is the octopus. Similar to the octopus, the system has many tentacles. As an internal coach, you will coach the individual tentacles, while also coaching the entire octopus. In other words, the internal coach is responsible for coaching the individuals and teams within the system, as well as the system as a whole.

Initial conversations

Include systemic coaching in your coaching agreement and initial conversations. It is important for all parties to understand that the scope of the internal coach's work includes coaching the system. By all parties, I am including the internal coach, the sponsor or department that has brought the internal coach in, and the top-tier of the organization's leadership.

It is essential that the top-tier of leadership within the organization understand that the scope of internal coaching includes the system, otherwise the overall impact and success of the coaching could be negatively affected. In fact, internal coach Cherie Silas commented that her experience is that 98% of the impact of internal coaching stops, or encounters sabotage, at the top-tier leadership level.

In addition to your initial conversations, include educating the leadership in systems thinking as an ongoing component of your work as an internal coach. Capitalize on teachable moments when you can ask leaders to share what they are noticing at the systemic level, while also sharing what you are noticing.

This chapter will provide a basic primer on systems thinking that coaches and leaders can use within their organizations. This will help leaders better understand the rationale of including systems coaching, as well as enable leaders themselves to begin to view their organization and its efforts and endeavors through a systems lens. The successful internal coach understands that there is a direct correlation between awareness and empowerment. Greater awareness equals greater empowerment.

Erkan suggested that one way to increase awareness of the system as a whole is to name the system or create a metaphor for the system. It is preferable that the leadership of the organization come up with the name or metaphor, although it will also work if the coach comes up with a name. This is a concrete way of seeing the system as a whole, as an individual unit. What I like about this suggestion is that at any point the system name or metaphor can be changed, which can be a catalytic moment for the system.

One final comment before moving forward on how to coach the system is that whether we recognize it or not, we are always working with systems, and the interplay between those systems. Both internal and external coaches are coaching an endless number of systems within systems—even temporary systems. Therefore, systemic coaching competence is a skill for all coaches.

Cherie invited me to learn more about systemic coaching by watching a series of videos that she has developed for her company, Tandem Coach Training Academy. Below is a brief synopsis of what Cherie shares with both new coaches and organizational leaders regarding systemic coaching. As an internal coach, she also shares this information with the organization's leaders.

Understanding roles and voices in systems

Every system contains roles. The internal coach needs to pay attention to three of those roles in particular: outer roles, inner roles, and hidden roles (sometimes called ghost voices).

Outer roles are the most obvious since they describe the external functions and titles of individuals within the system. Examples within an organization would include: supervisor, manager, administrator, CEO, and COO. Examples within a family unit would include: mother, father, aunt, uncle, and child. The outer roles describe a function or place within the system.

Inner roles are less obvious because they are the internal maintenance and relationship aspects of the system. Inner roles address the emotional health of the system. People within a system take on various roles within that system, which may or may not have anything to do with their outer role. Examples of inner roles include: devil's advocate, tension breaker, comforter, initiator, disturber, rule follower or breaker. It is important to understand that all of the inner voices are good and contribute to the system. Each inner role helps members to see things from different perspectives and is invaluable in keeping the system healthy.

Hidden roles, often affectionately referred to as ghost voices, remind the system of how things used to be, often including leftover sentimentality. They can also remind the system of a person who used to be there, who still has an influence on the system today. An example would be a former boss that everyone loved. The ghost gives voice as people compare a new boss to their former beloved boss, for example, "When so and so was here this didn't happen."

Ghost voices, like ghosts, keep haunting an organization and leadership. What's worse is the ghost voices can seem very real. Many years ago, in one of my first leadership roles, I frequently heard people reference "Bob," saying things like, "Bob would want us to ..." or "Bob wouldn't agree with this." What struck me as odd was that there wasn't a single Bob or Robert on the leadership team, or in the organization at large. Six months into my leadership role I finally asked, "Who is Bob and when will I get to meet him?" To my surprise, I was informed that Bob had died over a decade previously.

Other times, ghost voices aren't as overt, although you can feel them. Recent members to the system are especially sensitive to ghost voices. Sometimes this is referred to as the elephant in the room.

Coaching and working with roles

How do you coach with these roles? One of your initial steps is to educate individuals and teams on the three roles and how to recognize them within the system. This is another way the internal coach carries out the guiding principles of being an agent of awareness.

Cherie described a team that was in gridlock. Their communication was toxic and no one was addressing it, which was clearly one of many elephants in the room. The next time Cherie met with this particular team, she brought with her several paper cut-outs of elephants that were big, medium, and small.

She directed the group members to write one of the challenges they were experiencing within the group on a paper elephant, choosing the size of the elephant to match the magnitude of the challenge—small, medium, or large. In the weekly sessions that followed, one elephant was selected at random and addressed by the group.

This creative exercise added laughter and lightness to what had been a sensitive and avoided topic of discussion. Within a few weeks the group reported that they "got it," and going forward would address the elephants in the room.

In addition to educating and informing your clients about systems thinking, you will also want to coach them. While most people are familiar with their own outer role and those of others, there will be less awareness and more confusion about the other roles.

Outer roles

Helping individuals and teams get clear on job function to get their work done is a fairly straightforward coaching approach. Begin by identifying all the roles or job titles. Then, identify the various functions that need to be addressed and accomplished. Note that role title and job function do not always align. Encourage the team to discuss the following questions:

- What are the functions of each role and what are we expecting?
- What am I expecting? What are we as team members expecting? What are others expecting?
- What are the functions that are unassigned?
- Do we really need each function that we have identified?
- What functions are missing for us as a team?

Then, each team member answers the following questions:

- Do I have the ability and capability to do these roles?
- Where do we get the help?

Then, out of these discussions, set up working agreements with the team.

Inner roles

As part of a team exercise, suggest the team answer questions like:

- What are the current inner roles on our team?
- How is each of these roles attempting to be helpful?
- What would happen if we didn't have these inner roles on our team?
- What is frustrating us today about each particular inner role? (Consider asking the team member currently in this role to tell the group what it's like to fill the role. Remind them that they do not need to continue in their present inner role. They have a choice. Invite them to consider what inner role they really want.)
- As a team, what are the inner roles that we really need?
- How useful are each of these roles?
- How can these roles be skillfully delivered to our team?

As a team, develop written agreements as the team experiments with new inner roles.

Ghost roles

In addition to educating the team about ghost roles and reminding them that all systems have them, consider the following group process and questions:

- As a team, identify the ghosts present in the system. It's not necessary to name the people. What's of greater importance is naming the role or voice the ghost places within the system.
- How is this ghost role trying to be helpful? What is its purpose?
- Consider the impact each ghost is having on the team.
- How can the team honor the ghost? Honor what needs to be honored and bring forward what it's trying to do. Also, consider what needs to be forgiven and forgotten.
- As a team, consider what we are going to do with each ghost role. How can we ask it to leave? Or, how can we transfer the function of each ghost voice into the present? Who can we assign it to? How can we grieve what we have lost? What wisdom from the ghost voice do we need to draw from?
- Remind the team that the goal is to be present-driven not ghost-driven.
- What will we do if the ghost returns?
- Based on all of the above, what is our working agreement as a team?

Assessing the system

The purpose of assessing the system is to help the system understand who they are, as well as what they need. Cherie suggests a two-pronged approach when assessing the system:

1 A self-assessment by the system itself
2 An assessment by the internal coach.

The system's self-assessment

As the internal coach you can conduct a series of interviews with individuals, groups, and teams at varying levels and places within the organization. You can also expand the interview to include individuals and groups that interact with the organization, but are outside of the system. Interview questions to consider include:

- What have you seen done well over the past months?
- What areas, if focused on, would produce the biggest positive changes?
- What are your challenges and impediments? How does the organization contribute to your challenges? What's frustrating you?
- How do you view this organization overall? What is the culture like, i.e., leadership, morale, way of working?
- Describe the physical, cultural, and relational space of this organization.

Then, schedule a time to meet with the organizational leaders and team and share a summary of your findings. Use language like:

- Here's what I heard you say ...
- The top challenges/priorities you identified were ...
- Here's what those outside of your organization are saying ...
- As a result of these findings, what do you want to do?
- What do you want to tackle first?

The coach's assessment

Here's where it can get a bit tricky as the internal coach because you are part of the system and have a stake in the outcome. As the internal coach, you will want to adopt a coaching mindset and continue to ask questions, rather than making judgments. You will want to remind yourself that you are not here to fix the system, but rather to provide them with another perspective of their system.

Cherie suggests that, initially, you will want to be in observation mode. In this stage, you will want to get to know people and processes. Listening and noticing will be your primary objectives. When you do share your observations, your main role will be that of a mirror, helping the organization to see itself through an outside, neutral third-party lens.

Christine Thompson noted:

> "When I talk to a person, I'm watching for patterns in what they're saying to see if we can find something that they might not be aware of, a theme that's running through their life. And I find it the same when you're working with organizations, when you're talking to different people in a department. What themes are you seeing? What patterns are you seeing? What's the perception that everybody shares that's causing a problem? And what are the individual things that need to be treated differently?
>
> It's about finding those patterns and those themes and picking those out, and then holding the mirror up and saying, 'You guys are all telling me that Monday mornings are a nightmare in this organization. What's going on?' Just finding that thing and throwing it back. So observing, yes. Interviewing, yes. Looking for patterns and themes and reflecting that back."

Your primary coaching skills in this process will include: silence, listening, powerful questions, empathy, noticing, and acknowledging. As you report back to the organization, you will want to preface your noticing with phrases like:

- What I appreciate about you is ... You are breathing positivity into the system, giving credit to the system. You are helping them see clearly the attributes that they have.
- What I notice about you is, or what I'm wondering about is ... From a neutral, non-judgmental place, you are seeking to know more. You are helping them to become more aware of the inner working of their system.

In an interview with Cherie, coach Aanu Gopald offered her insights on implementing change within the system:

- Bringing change to a system is identical to coaching an individual in that it all begins with the relationship.
- Focus first on being non-judgmental and communicating empathy.
- Partner with people instead of trying to fix them.
- Be respectful of the individuals, teams, and the system.
- Your goal, as trust increases, is to help them discover for themselves what is really going on in the system.
- True to coaching, questions will be more helpful than answers.

In all of the coaching that you do, remember that you are not responsible for driving the change. Your client is in the driver's seat and you are in the passenger seat. The greatest value that you offer your client (individual, team, or system) is your unique view from the passenger seat. So, unless it's an absolute, irrecoverable emergency, keep your hands off of the steering wheel.

Unlike the driver, you do not need to keep your eyes focused ahead and you do not have the responsibility of operating any heavy machinery. The passenger seat affords you the opportunity to take a longer, deeper look at what's ahead, behind, and along the roadside. You can even take your eyes completely off the road to use another resource.

Richard Lister says:

"Analyze the culture of the organization that you're in. So if you have a leadership that is more directive in style, and you're an internal coach, that's quite a tricky challenge because you're kind of going against the flow. So part of what I've done in trying to spread coaching in our organization, informally, is think about which leaders would we want to come alongside and encourage into a more of a coaching way, in the hope that they would influence the senior leadership across the organization. Who are your allies? How can we work with them and then how can we talk about the stories of change?"

Some questions that an internal coach can ask themselves as they coach the system include:

- What best describes your team, group, and systems coaching? Hub-and-spoke or web?
- What name have you (or your client) given to the team or system you are coaching?
- When you first begin coaching with an organization, what are you noticing that others do not seem to notice?
- When you first started working here, what did you notice or question that you no longer notice or question?
- What roles (voices) in the system need to be heard?

Additional questions to consider:

- If you were to give a name to your organizational system, what would it be?
- What are you no longer aware of that you were keenly aware of when you first joined the team?
- Name one ghost voice within your organization. How is this ghost voice helpful? Unhelpful?

10 Guiding principle #7: Live with your mess

"I sometimes think of consultants and external coaches as 'seagull coaches.' The seagull flies in and leaves a deposit, and then it flies away. And they don't really live with the mess they make. For internal coaches, you have to live with the mess you make."

Vernon Stinebaker offered this interesting insight about internal coaching, saying that internal coaches "live with their mess." When an external coach is brought in, they do their work and then leave. The internal coach, on the other hand, does their work and stays, because they are part of the system. They live (and coach) in the mess that they are making.

Vernon continued:

"I think a corresponding analogy might be that people will execute in a certain way while we have the gun held to their head. But once the threat is no longer there, they'll go back to familiar, comfortable ways of working. [When internal coaches realize] that you're going to live with them, then you're investing a different amount of time and energy in those things.

I think a deeper understanding of going beyond individual culture and into group culture and group values is really important. It is important to develop rapport and understanding of your clients at the individual level. But whenever you move into a system where you have multiple individuals interacting with one another, the complexity is basically exponential, as the number of people increases, the channels of communication increase, the state of the market increases."

Vernon referred to the effects of something called the VUCA environment, which stands for volatility, uncertainty, complexity, and ambiguity. "The ability for coaches to help organizations guide themselves during states of relative calm in preparation for this kind of turmoil is really, really key," Vernon said. "And I think that deeper understanding of values and culture that comes from living in the mess is key to help build strong values that will help the organization stick together in times of extreme turbulence."

Viktor Glinka also commented on the benefits of living with your mess, saying that this offers the internal coach several unique advantages over the external coach. One of these advantages is that internal coaches essentially have more connections with their clients because they see them every day; they see their growth. Whereas when you're an external coach, you don't know what is going on between sessions.

The organization also benefits by having a coach living in their mess. It provides them with a pair of eyes that can be focused specifically on the system, while others can focus primarily on their day-to-day tasks at hand. And while this can be beneficial, it can also get uncomfortable and awkward.

The awkwardness and discomfort of living in your mess is a direct result of being in the midst of the daily decisions and changes being made by the organization. To put it another way, the external coach will typically see snapshots of major change and implementation at various points along the way, whereas the internal coach is seeing a livestream video of the implementation and change—while also being a character in the livestream drama. This can add pressure for the internal coach to always be on.

External coaches are often encouraged to forget about their clients in between sessions, which in a way sort of takes the pressure off. The internal coach rarely has that luxury.

Change is not a straight line

A wide variety of organizations benefit from having an internal coach living and coaching in their mess. Start-up businesses, for example. Start-ups experience a rapid pace of change, along with unexpected opportunities and obstacles, making easy access to a coach extremely beneficial. The fast-paced environment of a new venture warrants more than weekly or twice-monthly coaching sessions.

Many faith-based organizations would benefit from the on-the-spot coaching of the internal coach. The majority of today's faith-based organizations are experiencing a sharp decline in membership, participation, and fund development. Many are coming to terms with the reality that the traditional ways of meeting people's spiritual needs are not working, and they need to re-envision themselves. This re-envisioning process is, at its core, cultural, systemic change.

Change is not a straight line moving from where you are currently to where you want to be. Instead, change is a series of twists and turns, moving forward, backwards, and laterally on a daily, sometimes hourly basis. At any one of these twists and turns, our clients can stall, give up, default to previous behaviors, or become overwhelmed. Internal coaches, because they are living in the mess, are present at any and all of these points.

It is absolutely critical for the internal coach to know that they can empower or disempower at any of these moments. The masterful coach learns to discern when to step in and when to stay out.

Some questions that the internal coach can ask themselves at these critical moments include:

- Whose need am I responding to at this moment? Mine? Theirs?
- What does the organization/system need from me right now?

- How else might I respond?
- Who else can respond?
- What's at stake for me right now?
- When is it best for me to step in?

Additional questions to consider:

- Regarding the mess you are currently working in, what is one contribution that you can make *because* you are in the mess?
- What are the signs and signals that you need resources and support from someone *not* living in the mess?

11 Guiding principle #8: Confidentiality, yes. Secret-keeping, no!

During our interview, Geertruyt Stokes emphasized the importance of confidentiality. As part of her ongoing contracting process, she asks the following question: "What is confidential and what isn't confidential?" Cherie Silas agrees and adds that she also reminds her clients that she is not the secret keeper. "Yes, I keep confidence, but I don't keep secrets. Don't come tell me secrets about the rest of the team that you want me to keep."

These two seasoned internal coaches have highlighted an important distinction between confidentiality and secret-keeping. What we keep confidential, as the coach, are the private conversations and personal matters of our clients. These can include personal and professional ambitions, a strategic or tactical plan that your client has thought through with you, therapeutic and medical concerns, points of view and opinions, as well as family matters.

Geertruyt also raised the question of what to do when you hear information about other people in the organization. While the focus of confidentiality is on our client, the focus of secret-keeping is on others, when clients relay second-hand information and observations. Secrets show up in a variety of ways during coaching. They can at times be overt, when a client mentions something about another person or team outright.

Other times, an outside person can become the topic of the coaching conversation. When this happens, my response as a coach is to say, "That other person isn't here and so I can't coach them. You are here today and I can only coach you right now."

Telling secrets occurs for any number of reasons. For example, telling secrets can be an avoidance tactic, meant to deflect attention from oneself. It can also be an attempt to show power or demonstrate value and worth to others. The not-so-subtle message of the secret teller is, "I have important information that others do not have." Telling secrets is a way of "being in the know," or being privy to information that others do not have. It can also be as simple as a bad habit, closely aligned to gossip.

The problem with secrets

The problem with secret-keeping is that it does not move our clients and the organization they work within toward improved system health. Rather, it does the opposite. In many cases, secret-keeping creates triangulation and an unhealthy relationship dynamic; often, the result is intentional manipulation and miscommunication regarding an issue, challenge, or person.

Secret-keeping, and the resultant triangulating of relationships, has the potential to expand exponentially throughout the system. In other words, go viral. Once viral, instead of dealing with issues A, B, and C, secret-keeping adds an additional dimension to the interactions. This would be analogous to playing a regular game of chess versus a three-dimensional game of chess. There is so much more to consider.

In addition, secret-keeping takes up valuable time and energy of the coach. It can easily become muddled with the confidential information that the coach must not share. It can also entangle the coach in the interactions of two parties, and may even sway the coach's opinion of another individual. The bottom line is that secret-keeping does not promote healthy communication between individuals and groups.

Yet secrets often show up as a part of the regular coaching conversation. Consider the following coaching scenario in which the coach was working with an individual toward a promotion within the organization. Simultaneously, the coach was also coaching her client's manager. At one point in the coaching conversation, the manager disclosed that there was a strong possibility that the other client she was coaching was going to be terminated. The coach is now the keeper of a secret and facing the dilemma of a conflict of interest.

This scenario happens frequently for the internal coach and requires the coach to be constantly on the lookout for potential conflicts of interest, while also regularly re-negotiating their coaching agreements with their clients.

Getting the story into the open

One of the helpful and healthy strategies that I use with organizations to address secrets, as well as other forgotten information, is to have the organization create a timeline. Ideally, the timeline begins when the organization came into being, and continues to the present day. (In advance of the group gathering, I usually cover the walls of a large room with newsprint and have already written on the newsprint the start date and the current date, with a long horizontal line connecting the two.)

With the group members present I invite them to add significant dates and stories to the timeline. Sometimes pre-work is needed for this timeline to be thorough. Once everything is listed on the timeline, as a group we walk the timeline and talk about the stories and memories passed down at various points along the timeline. I often find that the creation story is incredibly valuable, even if the current state of affairs is radically different. Other key events may also come to the surface. And yes, many secrets are shared, in ways that can help the current leadership.

The coaches I interviewed offered several suggestions relating to potential conflicts of interest and secret-keeping:

- Resist the urge to be in perpetual coaching relationships. Be sure to define a start time, as well as an end time. You can always contract for more time, if needed. Also, be clear in defining what they want to accomplish and what is your role.
- Remember, you're not really neutral, because you are part of the system. The question is not *if* you will encounter conflicts of interest, rather *when* you will encounter them. You may have a different opinion or point of view than your boss about the team or individual that you are coaching.
- To the best of your ability, identify the potential conflicts of interest and then be explicit about them with the people you're working with in your coaching agreement and design around them. For example, you could say: "I just spent a year coaching the person that you're having problems with."
- Resist the trap that you are the coach to everyone. Erkan Kadir ran into a situation where he was coaching a team, and the leader of that team—and his sponsor in the organization—would continually come to him for coaching. "Well, hold on a second," he said, "I can't be your coach because I am representing the interests of the organization. I can't be your messenger. I had to say the same thing to the leadership team. The coaching I did with that team was powerful! Man, did they move forward. And it really could've only happened if I didn't let myself fall into the trap of being a coach to everyone who asks, without considering who I'm supposed to be coaching."

One final comment: while the majority of secret-keeping is not helpful or healthy, there are times when secrets need to be shared. For example, when inappropriate behavior or illegal activity occurs, those secrets need to be shared with the appropriate person or department. In these cases, the role of the coach is to request that the client share this with the appropriate person.

Some questions the internal coach could ask themselves when dealing with confidentiality and secret-keeping include:

- What is confidential? What isn't?
- How can I best educate my clients around confidentiality and secret-keeping?
- What will I do with the secrets people have told me?
- How can I keep the secrets I've been told from influencing me?
- What do I do that encourages people to tell me secrets?

Additional questions to consider:

- How are secrets showing up in your organization? What's the impact?
- What secrets need to remain secrets?
- Who do you know that responds to secrets in a healthy, helpful way? What can you learn from them?

12 Guiding principle #9: Who coaches the coach?

Because as an internal coach you are part of the system, it is a challenge to leave yourself at the door and not get caught up in the inevitable conflicts of interest we discussed in the previous guiding principle. Raquel Silva warns internal coaches not to let themselves become "institutionalized" by their role. It is a danger for them to get absorbed by internal politics and the dos and the don'ts of the system, and instead they need to learn how to stay neutral.

Christine Thompson advocates that we be very much aware of our assumptions and triggers—in other words, the internal coach must do their own work. Miriam Cheuk agrees:

> "Everything you're doing or not doing on a daily basis is contributing to whether or not people are going to trust you. You can't be a true coach if you do not model the things you're asking of others. What's key is how you're showing up, and that you continue to do your own development when you're trying to help others."

Pradeepa Narayanaswamy also advocates for the grounding that regular coaching and supervision provide the internal coach. We need to be grounded for the work that we do. Geertruyt Stokes points out that the system is unhealthy—that's why you are there—and the coach is very much in danger of being pulled into that culture of blaming and other harmful behaviors.

Viktor Glinka says that when he was quite new to his role as an internal coach,

> "I was often confused and distracted by my internal dialogue. I would ask myself, 'am I doing it right?' Mentor-coaching and supervision sessions really helped me to leave that voice behind and become more sensitive to my instinct. Now, it is not a matter of doing it right, rather it is all about being in the moment with my client."

Always be growing

Continuous improvement and learning is key in coaching, noted Syed Ali. Keep studying new books and coaching models, he says, and agile concepts to keep you up to date. Then you can share your thoughts, challenges, and learnings with the community in a blog or on social media.

We always need to be growing as coaches, noted Richard Lister. "Are we being supervised? Is our practice being reviewed? And are we being nudged into places where we're being challenged?"

About her experience as a coaching client, Pradeepa said,

> "When I see myself grow, I take that growth and start helping my clients go even deeper as well. So it will reflect on my coaching when my growth happens.
>
> I don't just talk the talk; I walk the walk. I always encourage people to have their own coach. Find somebody to help you with your own blind spots, to show the mirror back to you so that you are also constantly growing. This is what has really helped me stay grounded and be confident in what I bring to the table."

I agree wholeheartedly with all of these viewpoints. In my experience, there's a direct correlation between the growth of the coach and the growth of the client. During my first eight years of coaching I worked three times per month with a mentor-coach.

Over the past twelve years I have continued my growth by always working with a coach, sometimes a business development coach, other times a personal life coach, and more recently another coach for supervision.

In addition to being actively engaged with another coach for my continued growth and grounding, I have also been intentional to meet regularly with my peers. I have a variety of peer coaches—PCC and MCC—who I collaborate with on projects and curriculum development. While these are informal connections, they do provide me with direct input and critique from others.

The ICF (International Coaching Federation) encourages coaches to be actively engaged in coaching supervision and communities of practice. And I would strongly encourage internal coaches to consider a recent article in the *International Coaching Psychology Review* (Volume 12, No. 1, March 2017), which identifies these key benefits for coaches who receive coaching supervision:

- Increased self-awareness
- Greater confidence
- Increased objectivity
- Heightened sense of belonging
- Reduced feelings of isolation
- Increased resourcefulness.

The ICF states that the coaching supervision process may include:

- Exploring the coach's internal process through reflective practice
- Reviewing the coaching agreement and any other psychological or physical contacts, both implicit and explicit

- Uncovering blind spots
- Ethical issues
- Ensuring the coach is "fit for purpose" and perhaps offering accountability
- Looking at all aspects of the coach and client's environment for opportunities for growth in the system.

The importance of supervision is noted in other coaching organizations as well, for example:

- The European Mentoring and Coaching Council (EMCC Global). EMCC recommends that coaches/mentors should undertake no less than 1 hour of supervision per 35 hours of practice, ensuring a minimum of 4 hours per year.
- International Association of Coaching (IAC). The IAC does not *require* supervision or mentor hours for IAC certification, but support from mentors or participation in study groups is highly recommended.
- The Association for Professional Executive Coaching (APECS). Prospective certified coaches are required to have a minimum of five years of personal experience receiving executive business, as well as evidence of and commitment to continuing personal professional development including self-awareness and supervision.

Coaches would also benefit from participation in communities of practice where they can receive and share best practices, trends, tools, and tips. One resource for communities of practice is the International Coaching Federation website, where you will find an up-to-date list.

Participation in an ICF community of practice is free of charge to all members in good standing. At the time of the writing, there was a community of practice specifically for internal coaches. The benefit of participating in an ICF community of practice is that you will be involved in a live discussion on relevant topics, as well as interact with coaches from around the world.

Other sources for a community of practice would include your local ICF chapter and the accredited school where you received your coach training. In our coach program, we encourage our students to connect with each other outside of class and to continue this practice after graduation. Years after graduating we have had numerous students tell us that they still meet regularly with former classmates.

I have one final thought about this topic of who coaches the coach. I've heard motivational speaker Jim Rohn state that we are the average of the five people we spent the most time with. Rohn further explained that the people we surround ourselves with and the people we pay attention to matters. It can be the difference between challenging ourselves to be our very best or coasting along and just getting by.

That's what this guiding principle is all about. The successful internal coaches that I interviewed were intentional at including a coach, or other professional, in their inner circle of five so that they could be their very best. I strongly recommend the same for each person reading this book.

When considering the topic of who coaches the coach, I would encourage internal coaches to consider the following questions:

- Who are the five people that you spend the most time with?
- What impact are the five people having on you, personally and professionally?
- What one or two individuals, if added, would have the most dramatic impact on you?
- What's your strategy to stay grounded?
- Who can best help you stay grounded?
- Who have you given permission to provide you with candid, healthy feedback?

Additional questions to consider:

- What additional steps can your organization initiate to promote the ongoing personal and professional growth of its members?
- What additional resources and actions do leadership need to identify for this to become a reality?
- What absolutely needs to change or end for this to happen?

13 Guiding principle #10: Demonstrate your worth

One of the strongest themes to emerge from my conversations with internal coaches for this book was the topic of demonstrating your worth. Those I interviewed reiterated time and time again that demonstrating the value that coaching provides an organization is typically overlooked or it is assumed that the value of coaching is obvious to all—including the decision-makers.

Brock Argue commented that one of the biggest challenges for internal coaches is quantifying the value of their coaching. Every year organizations look at their vision and take stock and set new plans in place. If the decision-makers, often not the ones that you are coaching, do not easily see the value of coaching, there is a risk that coaching will not be included in any new plans.

Geertruyt Stokes says that the internal coach needs to connect to the bigger purpose of the organization. There is a whole play happening between the internal coach, HR, and the business goals and objectives. You, as the internal coach, need to be asking yourself: How do I connect what I do as a coach, and the results that I bring, with the organization's new goals?

Clearly, internal coaches need to be spending a much greater percentage of their time and energy:

- educating the organization's members about what coaching is,
- communicating the success stories of coaching, and
- quantifying data that makes visible the benefits of coaching to their organization.

Erkan Kadir explained that successful internal coaches are well adept at demonstrating each of the above. They understand that these are just as much a part of the job description of the internal coach as is the actual coaching of individuals and teams. Let me elaborate further on each of the above.

Educating the organization's members about what coaching is

Erkan commented that many people are still asking, "What the heck is coaching?" People may struggle to define coaching because it is relatively new, because the coaching mindset is focused on the client's expertise instead of that of the coach—which seems counterintuitive—or because as coaches we have done a poor job of communicating what coaching is. Regardless of the reason, it is our responsibility as coaches to bridge this communication gap.

Years ago, I heard a coach say that people do not invest in or buy what they do not understand. It is a tall order to expect an organization to invest in something as elusive as coaching.

It is our job to help others understand coaching and its inherent value. Therefore, the educational process of helping people understand coaching is not a once-and-done process. It is ongoing and repeated often. We cannot assume that because we have told someone what coaching is, they will remember. Plus, the regular turnover of employees in any organization will always provide us with a new group to educate.

Communicating the success stories of coaching

Alex Sloley explained that the accomplishments of the internal coach need to be visible. While the direct client experiences the benefit of coaching firsthand, others may not. Or, if a manager sees significant improvement in someone, they may not attribute the improvement to coaching.

Alex highlights for us the delicate balance of confidentiality and visibility. Internal coaches need to learn how to tell the story of the impact and influence of coaching in responsible and ethical ways. Richard Lister considers one of the roles of the internal coach to be that of storyteller. Coaches may, with client permission, share coaching stories—making sure they are sanitized.

We can obtain written testimonials directly from our clients. When we set up triangle coaching agreements between client, manager/sponsor, and coach, we can agree in advance about what can and cannot be shared.

As an added challenge, says Brock, you may have clearly communicated to your immediate boss or supervisor what coaching is and the value you have added, but your immediate supervisor then needs to be able to communicate that to their supervisor or board. You've got to help them help you!

A manager spoke to Brock about this challenge: "I know that coaching works. I know it's beneficial. It feels like the right thing to do to have a coach. I need you to give me something quantifiable, hard numbers or something that I can tell everyone else. I'm getting pressure from them [his immediate supervisors] about the value of coaching."

Internal coaches need to remember that there is an entire organization above the managers and supervisors that you work directly with that may not understand what coaching is and the value it brings. Internal coaches need to target that group of decision-makers in their educational attempts.

Quantifying the data that makes visible the benefits of coaching to their organization

According to Erkan, quantifying your value can be as simple as writing down a list of the objectives that you helped people achieve and then polling them afterwards. "How much of this would you attribute to coaching? What kind of value would you place on it? How close did we get to meeting your objectives?" Their answers can help you pull numbers out and you can give those numbers to the leaders to justify their investment in coaching.

Richard said,

> "I think there's something about the stories. I analyzed my coaching according to areas that I work on, and I might have something that says, 'Has the coaching increased your effectiveness in your job or improved your working relationships or—?' And then you can get some statistics and you could say, 'Okay, so twenty-two managers in the organization have been polled and 72% of them record an improvement in their effectiveness. And this many have seen a reduction in interpersonal conflict.'"

In discussing coaching the system and championing a coaching approach, Richard also suggested you consider who your allies are in the organization, those who have seen the benefits of coaching. How can we work with them and then how can we talk about the stories of change? He noted that while it's a challenge because of confidentiality, if we can mix stories together—i.e., create a composite, and change names—we need to be providing that information to nudge the leadership to adopt a change in approach.

Another approach from Erkan is to use a rating scale of 1 to 10 (1 being poor and 10 being excellent) at the beginning of the coaching engagement and then again at the end of the engagement, asking each team member to rate things like, "How is your communication as a team?" Collate the before and after ratings and you now have quantifiable data that you can share.

During my conversation with Brock, I shared that I spend about 30% of my time as an external coach keeping my pipeline full. In other words, demonstrating the worth of coaching. Brock commented that 30% would be a benchmark for internal coaches to aspire to but at best he estimates internal coaches are spending 10% of their time on demonstrating their worth. Allison Pollard confirms this guesstimate by commenting, "I'm loving your number of 30%. I'm usually at 10–20%."

Aligning yourself with what HR is doing

An often overlooked strategy for demonstrating your worth is to align yourself with HR. They are one of the groups that can be your biggest advocate. And if you are aligned with what's important to HR, it will increase your visibility and HR will become a natural spokesperson as to your worth as a coach to the upper levels of leadership—who likely haven't a clue about coaching, or you!

Geertruyt suggests,

> "Sit down with HR, be clear about what your role is and isn't, get their support. The company needs to be trained, not just you, but there is a whole

systemic way of looking at it. Who all needs to be aware, who all needs to be trained? Am I just going to be the one person that people can come to who want the coaching, or am I going to be deployed?

What's the story here? What's the story of me doing this work, and why is the company willing to pay for this? Great, then how will you support me so that we, together, make that happen?"

She says this conversation needs to happen not just with Human Resources (HR), but also possibly with senior management. You want to get this systemic support so that they will introduce you, that they will speak well of you, that they will tell you, "Please come to my management team and coach me," and model that to others.

You may need to train other internal coaches, and educate them about what internal coaching is, and HR needs to help with that. "You might not be the one person who puts down all the boundaries because, before you know it, people don't like you anymore because you're supposed to be the nice person. So the system has to help you with that."

You also need to be aligned with whatever people development initiatives HR is doing, so you speak the same language and you don't end up doing something completely different. "Make sure that you're systemically connected with whatever else is happening in the company."

Some questions that the internal coach can ask themselves so that they are regularly demonstrating their worth include:

- How much time do you devote to demonstrating your worth as a coach? 5%? 10%? 30%?
- How is what you do as a coach directly connected with the goals of the organization?
- What is your single-sentence definition of what coaching is?
- When was the last time you quantified your coaching data?
- What's the story you are telling yourself about demonstrating your worth as a coach?
- How frequently do you engage in conversations with HR and their goals and needs?

Additional questions to consider:

- What will it take to ensure that top-tier leadership regularly hears about the significant contribution coaching is making to the organization?
- What data, if tracked before and after coaching, would be most convincing to the decision-makers?
- What steps can HR and Leadership and Development (L&D) take to further cement the partnership they have with their internal coaches?

14 Guiding principle #11: Give conflict a voice

Over the past several decades, the questions that we have been asking about conflict have been evolving. Pre-1980s we were asking: How do we resolve conflict? The past several decades we've been asking: How do we manage conflict? Today's internal coaches are guided by an entirely different question: How do we give conflict a voice?

Internal coaches recognize that there is conflict in the system and that the voice of healthy conflict needs to be turned up louder for the benefit of the system, as well as its individual members. Cherie Silas stated: "Coaches need to get really comfortable with conflict. You can't be your best without conflict."

Most people and systems want to run away from conflict, primarily because they have only known toxic, unhealthy conflict. Those you coach either want to avoid conflict at all costs, or they are overly invested in the conflict and want to win at all costs. One of the roles of the internal coach is to help people recognize that there is both unhealthy and healthy conflict. When conflict occurs within the system, we ought to recognize and encourage healthy conflict, because conflict is a signal that something new is attempting to show up.

The problem with fixing conflict

When different ideas and perspectives rub against each other, it causes conflict. A typical response is to ask the leader to settle the dispute in an attempt to have all parties fall back in line. The problem with this approach is that it discourages and squelches new ideas and innovation. It also forces people to internalize the energy they feel regarding the conflict, as opposed to getting the energy out in a healthy manner.

This internalized energy doesn't simply dissipate, rather it festers and grows, often released at another moment of conflict. When the squelched conflict is finally released, along with the new in-the-moment conflict, it compounds everything. A frequent response is, "Where did all this anger come from? It seems much more than is necessary for this present conflict." As the internal coach, we want to "poke the beehive," encouraging healthy conflict to bring forth ideas.

Of course, training and modeling of healthy conflict prior to "poking the beehive" is strongly recommended, for example non-violent communication or a discussion of the book *Crucial Conversations*.

Madhavi Ledalla recommends using the SCARF model when coaching teams, developed by David Rock of the NeuroLeadership Institute. His research and ongoing work is based on the brain's sense that other people's actions either put us in danger (we experience a threat) or keep us safe and happy (we experience a reward).

SCARF stands for the five domains of threat and reward that influence our behavior in social situations. These are:

Status – the drive we feel to stand out from the crowd
Certainty – for our roles and responsibilities to be clear
Autonomy – our sense of control over the work that we do
Relatedness – the sense that we belong
Fairness – a sense of equity and equality.

Rock's research implies that these five social domains activate the same threat and reward responses in our brain that we rely on for physical survival. How we react to these perceived threats and rewards affects our emotions and behavior in the face of conflict.

We want our clients to not be afraid of conflict. Our role is to help individuals recognize where they are with conflict and examine their history with conflict, and to help the system as a whole see how it relates to conflict.

Giving conflict a voice—stories

Several years ago, I was asked to provide both individual and team coaching to the leadership team of a very large church. The rationale for coaching was the increasing negative comments and passive aggressive behavior by significant numbers of long-term members toward the current leadership team. The initial thinking by the leadership team was that the reason for this recent eruption was the dramatic increase in new members within the congregation and significant proposed additions in program offerings and budgeted expenses.

As the coaching unfolded, several strategies were developed to address the issues at hand, which resulted in limited success. As a last-ditch effort, one team member blurted out, "Why don't we just give people a chance to talk with us!" This led to the scheduling of a town hall-style listening event.

To the surprise of the team, the scheduled listening event was full to capacity. Extra chairs needed to be brought in. As promised, the team did not drive the agenda, rather they adopted a listening posture. Those gathered were given the floor to speak and after an awkward pause, individuals within the audience began speaking and continued non-stop for more than ninety minutes.

During the wrap-up time, the church members shared the major insight from this listening event for them was that their frustration had nothing to do with the current leadership team, but rather was left over from a leadership decision made twenty or more years earlier. This was not the first time a major growth in membership had occurred. Twenty years earlier similar growth pains were felt. At that time, the leadership team made an across-the-board decision for the entire church and squelched any and all attempts for people to express their frustration.

So, the frustration of years earlier had been festering and finally came to the surface. Only after it was given a voice could this team and organization begin to move toward a healthy future.

Contrast the above example with a team that I am currently coaching. This current team includes the principal members of a twenty-year-old company in which the sole remaining founding member is preparing to retire and exit the team. The founding leader has delayed his exit on several occasions, citing sustainability issues that only he can address.

During my individual interviews with the other principals, each shared their frustration with the founding principal and his ineffectiveness and inability to communicate with the others on the team. They all believed that the founding principal was negatively impacting the business and that his exit was long overdue. During the subsequent principal team meeting, I shared a summary of my interviews and that a recurring theme had been the principal member's exit strategy and timing. As a group, I then asked them to say more.

What followed was some candid conversation—heated at times—about the exit strategy and how to best handle any potential sustainability issues. By poking the beehive, this team was able to give voice to the conflict at hand and begin to move the company forward in a healthy manner.

Practical suggestions for conflict and "poking the beehive"

Get comfortable with conflict. Do your own work with conflict. It's not enough to read books and attend training events on conflict. You have to do your own personal conflict work. I strongly recommend working with your coach, or other helping professional, on your personal history with conflict.

For example, it can be helpful to understand how your family of origin addressed conflict. There are various assessment tools that can also shed light on your conflict style. Most recently, the EQ tool provided me with helpful information as to next steps for me in this area. In addition to knowing your conflict style, I strongly suggest that you address any past or current conflict in your life, especially conflict that was squelched. It will come to the surface and impact your coaching when you least expect it.

Maintain a neutral stance when coaching on conflict. Don't take sides. This can be very difficult, especially since you are part of the system that is in conflict. Pay attention to your whole being, including your body. Learn the early signs and signals that alert you that you are moving out of a neutral stance. I regularly remind myself that I lessen my effectiveness and the overall success of the group when I take sides. For a coach, taking sides is like kryptonite to Superman.

Encourage every voice to speak about conflict. My way of making sure that every voice is heard is to have a roster of everyone's names. As each person speaks, I place a small mark next to their name. This provides me with an easy reference as to who has spoken and who hasn't.

It's not unusual for people not to want to speak up in the larger group or to have their opinion identified. In these situations, I distribute sticky notes and ask people to write their opinion anonymously and then stick their note to the wall. After each person has placed their note on the wall, I suggest that, as a group, we literally "read the handwriting on the wall."

This levels the playing field and gives each voice and opinion equal weight. In many cases, what is discovered with this exercise is that the loudest voices did not represent the overall group opinion or thoughts.

Remember that conflict is the system revealing itself. Ask questions, notice and listen for what the system is trying to reveal. Invite those you coach to do the same. In theory, the majority of us will agree; in practice though, it's often a different story altogether. Here is where the value of doing your personal conflict work, and providing opportunities for others to do the same, will really pay off. Instead of the usual *fight-flight-freeze* response to conflict, what we want is a huge dose of curiosity to show up.

Some questions that the internal coach can ask themselves about conflict include:

- How did your family of origin deal with conflict?
- What is your current relationship with conflict?
- Who do you know that has a healthy relationship with conflict? What can you learn from them?
- What is one thing you can do to become more comfortable with conflict and the act of poking the beehive?

Additional questions to consider:

- How does your organizational system typically deal with conflict—*fight*, *flight*, or *freeze*?
- Identify one current conflict within your organizational system and give it a voice. What is it attempting to say?
- What is one long-ago conflict that still needs to be addressed?

15 Cultural considerations

While I am including this chapter on culture in a book on internal coaching, the topic is equally applicable to external coaches. Culture matters! It is important for coaches to be aware of and sensitive to the culture of those we coach. We also need to recognize that there will be times when the core root issue of those we coach is cultural rather than behavioral.

Consider this scenario:

Many years ago, I coached Tom, a pastor whose governing board required him to work with a coach. The odd thing was that Tom had been a stellar pastor in previous settings and was only at his new setting for five months.

During our first session, in which Tom was eight minutes late, I asked him why he was being required to work with a coach. Tom said, "I don't know. I give 110% and am always working hard." I noticed that Tom was more than five minutes late for each of our next two sessions.

Before we began our third session, I asked Tom about being late, to which he responded, "I am? Really. I hadn't noticed." When I asked Tom to look at a clock, he replied that he didn't wear a watch and there were no clocks in his office. I asked Tom, who was calling me from his mobile phone, to get up and find the nearest clock. Several minutes later, from the other end of the building, he gave me the correct time.

I followed up by asking Tom about what he knew about his current church and their sense of time. There was a long pause, followed by a subtle a-ha. Tom informed me that they were German in background and were extremely punctual. In fact, I've been told that if you arrive on time at this church, you are late. I followed up by asking Tom what he had just discovered.

The focus of our remaining coaching conversation was on time, culture, and its impact on his leadership. Very quickly Tom pulled together a plan to address his new understanding of time. Two weeks later, at our next coaching session, Tom reported raving reviews from his congregation. He said that the only person still upset was his wife. Tom said, "My wife is mad at you." I said, "Why? I haven't even met her." To which Tom replied, "She's been telling me for years to get a watch and to be more sensitive to time. And after paying you for coaching, I changed within three weeks."

Cultural considerations

Do your homework

Ask questions about cultural values and practices before beginning work with a new group. Review resources and speak with people who can inform you about cultural differences. For example, prior to my first trip to Brazil, my host told me that it would be important that I let people hug me. Brazilians, she said, are very touchy and huggy people. I so appreciated knowing this in advance, especially since in my culture we refrain from hugging.

Prior to my first visit to South Korea, I asked about and learned many key cultural facts. First, that the instructor is held in the highest of regard, and therefore rarely are questions asked or teachings challenged. That meant that during training events I would have to ask specific individuals to respond to my questions.

I was also told that age matters, and that the younger Korean students would be reluctant to ask me questions or challenge me as an older person. This showed up when I asked one of the participants in the coach training to coach me. He was younger, and gracefully declined. Also, I learned that Americans are much more comfortable with eye contact than Asians.

Gender is culture

Let me offer another example of cultural differences where the participants were all from the same culture. The difference was gender. Recently my training organization (Coaching4Today'sLeaders) was invited by Dr HiRho Park, PCC to facilitate several training events called *Women Coaching Women*.

The idea behind these training events was that women respond and develop differently when interacting with other women, as opposed to men. During two of the training events, I was the only male at the event among a group of fifty women leaders. My role was to facilitate the coach training and to do my best to become an honorary woman throughout the training.

In preparation for these events, I asked Dr Park what I could expect and for any guidance. She proved to be a wealth of information. She explained that women behave differently when there are men in the room, often hesitating to respond, thereby giving the men the first chance to respond—even when they know the answer. Plus, add to this that it is not unusual for men to interrupt women while speaking.

She also explained that women often feel a sense of responsibility for the event, which men do not. Without men, women often report being more relaxed and confident. Then Dr Park suggested that it would be very important, as the only male at the event, for me not to be a "typical male," and most importantly not to interrupt the women while they were speaking.

Throughout both *Women Coaching Women* training events, I observed women behaving exactly as Dr Park had told me. What I found interesting was that I had facilitated other events in which several of the women had been in attendance and they were quite different at the *Women Coaching Women* event. The only difference was that the previous events were attended by both men and women.

Seeing the differences

Coach Doris Dalton, the Director of Leadership Development & Intercultural Competency for the New York Conference of the United Methodist Church, shared her insights about cultural considerations for coaches:

"Much of culture lies beneath what we usually observe, and is expressed through values, concepts, and beliefs, such as cultural perspectives on conflict, authority, leadership styles, and how we relate to community. When we work with clients, we need to pay attention to the way they respond to cultural differences in their settings. Cultural differences may lead to different experiences of the same situation. If we are not attentive to this fact, we may minimize those different experiences, or worse, miss them all together.

For example, Judy was frustrated at the beginning of our coaching session. She is a white female pastor and serves on a diverse committee for her denomination. At a recent meeting, a Chinese male pastor stood to speak on an issue. Judy felt some of his points were incorrect, and needed to be addressed. She said she felt that, as a leader, it was her role and responsibility to respond.

Though she was a bit nervous to take such a stand, she stood to speak and shared her responses. There was no response or acknowledgement from the Chinese pastor, and after the meeting he would not speak with Judy. She said she was frustrated because she believed she did the right thing, but still felt the Chinese pastor did not understand her point.

I asked her to name the possible cultural differences in communication styles between her and the other pastor. After naming several differences, she paused. 'Oh, I see! As a white woman, I felt I was being a strong leader to stand up and boldly state my response. As a Chinese man, he may have felt he was being chastised like a child in front of his peers, and not treated with respect as another leader.'

When I asked her what she could have done differently with this response, she said she could have spoken to him privately after the meeting. She still would have the opportunity to make her point, and have productive dialogue with the pastor.

We are all impacted by implicit bias and socially constructed stereotypes about race, ethnicity, and gender. You may have done your own work to undo implicit bias and stereotypes from your thinking by educating yourself and participating in implicit bias training. However, identifying stereotypes and dismantling our implicit bias is a constant work.

One of the gifts of coaching is being able to help those we coach to discover how their unrealized implicit bias may impede their growth. It is silly to suggest that if you are coaching someone who is a Black man, for example, you should read about the experiences of Black men to get a greater understanding of what your coachee may be going through. I find that if someone who is white doesn't quite 'get it,' people of color will take a silent mental note, and keep going, but never extend trust that deeply again.

When coaching those who may be different from you in gender, racially, and ethnically, it is important that you establish yourself as someone who is safe and can be trusted.

Check your assumptions, ask curious questions, and listen with empathy ..."

Expect surprises

Even though you have done your homework and attempted to understand culture, expect surprises. I noticed during my first visit to South Korea that the women were always running to open the door for me. (For context, I grew up in a culture where men open doors for women.) It was an interesting exchange as we fought to open the doors for each other. I asked my host about this, to which she replied, "Oh, that's an old Korean custom. Women open the doors for men."

Even though there will be surprises along the way, enjoy learning a different way. You will be a better coach, and more importantly a better person, as you experience and appreciate various cultures.

Be incredibly respectful

Of utmost importance, be respectful of culture and practices that are different from your own. There is no right or wrong way – just different ways. I have learned that deep respect for people will cover a multitude of mistakes on my part.

Working with a translator

If you are coaching individuals who speak a different language, work with your translator ahead of time. Your translator will make or break your coaching experience, so it's important to build a relationship with them. Ideally, I like to arrange several phone conversations or detailed email exchanges in advance of any coaching.

What's most important is they're fluent in both languages and they understand what you're trying to accomplish with coaching.

Note that it is different coaching a group through a translator. The pace takes getting used to, as you'll need to pause while the interpreter translates your message. A translator can also give you insights into what to expect and important cultural considerations.

Culture matters

Keep in mind that even within one culture, there may be multiple subcultures and things that are true for people in one age group could be the opposite for another. There are some online resources and books that can give you a quick snapshot of a culture, but I still recommend talking to someone who lives there.

Vernon Stinebaker shared these insights from his twenty-five years of coaching in China:

"There are aspects of Asian culture that are very hierarchical. And in many Asian cultures, including China, the idea of the nail that's sticking out is the one that's going to be hammered down. Whereas, for example, in the West, I think we appreciate and encourage people to be vocal and to stand out, right, to demonstrate their difference. That's often perceived much differently here.

So you have to give people the space that they can move there on their own. And I think patience is an important part of that. Of course, like elsewhere in the world, I think that the culture is shifting. I think that there is more impatience here now than there used to be. And I think that with younger people who are exposed to a broader set of ideas and different technologies that enable those ideas, I think that there's maybe a little bit more blending amongst younger individuals than you might see in people who are a bit older. But in a general sense still, culture doesn't change as quickly as one might expect. And so I think giving people plenty of space so that they can move into that space of their own accord is really important.

[In a coaching context] I think that silence is an important opportunity for people to investigate and move into that space. So I think that having that kind of quietness and reflection is there. I think it's always important, of course, that the coach know the coachee at a deeper level.

A lot of the people that I work with are very analytical, in the IT industry. And so the way they come at things from that analytical perspective, you may want to encourage them to challenge themselves with data that will help them investigate directions. But there's also across Asia, I think, very long and deep kinds of spiritual traditions, as well. And so it's about inviting people that might be more inclined in those areas to investigate that. So a lot of coaching happens outside of the coaching session. And so again, helping people establish structures that are going to be useful for them in their development.

And so I think something that's been emerging a lot globally over the last few years is mindfulness in leadership. And, of course, many of those mindfulness practices come from Asia. India and China have thousands of years of mindfulness practices of various sorts. And so I think, for some people, those become an interesting opportunity for them to move into that white space, to rediscover things about themselves and their culture that can be meaningful at many different levels.

To me, perhaps one of the most fascinating things about coaching is the layers that are involved there. It seems like the infinite onion. There always seems to be more that we can discover about ourselves and others. To me, a great day is when I've had one or more of the people that I'm working with feel like they've peeled back another layer and have this new discovery of themselves."

A final note

What I have written regarding culture also applies to race, gender, gender preference, nationality, education, and economic status. Mutual respect is a core value for all coaches in every conversation that we encounter.

I can't imagine having a coaching business limited just to a single country anymore. The world is just too small and there is too much to appreciate. I do believe that coaching spans and can be adapted across different cultures. I've seen it happen. Give it time. Enjoy meeting people, and have fun!

16 Resources for internal coaches

Books

1 *The Five Dysfunctions of the Team: A Leadership Fable* by Patrick Lencioni, recommended by Vernon Stinebaker.
2 *Crucial Conversations: Tools for Talking When Stakes are High*, 2nd edition, by Kerry Patterson, Joseph Grenny, Ron McMillan, and Al Switzler, recommended by Mauricio Robles.
3 *Executive Coaching with Backbone and Heart: A Systems Approach to Engaging Leaders with Their Challenges*, 2nd edition, by Mary Beth O'Neill, recommended by Allison Pollard.
4 *The Coaching Habit: Say Less, Ask More & Change the Way You Lead Forever* by Michael Bungay Stanier, recommended by Vernon Stinebaker.

Questions to ask clients

Every coach has their favorite set of questions they reach for time and again. Several of the coaches I interviewed shared theirs with me, and some elaborated about how and why they use a particular question. I've included my favorites as well.

Val Hastings:

1 On a scale of 1 to 10 (1 = not ready, 10 = ready), how ready are you to begin the coaching process?
2 What's off limits?
3 What do you need from me? From others?
4 What is the story you are telling yourself?
5 What are the pain points that you are trying to solve?
6 What are you actually trying to solve?
7 What do you want to tackle first?
8 How do you want to start?
9 What have you seen done well over the past months?
10 What areas, if focused on, would produce the biggest positive change?
11 What are your challenges and impediments? How does the organization contribute to your challenges? What's frustrating you?

Alex Sloley:

1 How can I help you today?
2 What did we talk about last time?
3 What are you planning on doing?
4 Can you show me? (When I am getting them to visualize stuff)

Allison Pollard:

1 What is the goal? What would you like to have happen?
2 How would we know if [change] is working?
3 What would be a small step forward to help you learn?
4 How can you build upon what's working or your strengths?
5 How could you make things better by Friday?

Brock Argue:

1 What's on your mind?
2 What's the biggest challenge here for you?
3 What would you like to have happen?
4 What's in your way? / What's preventing you from moving forward? / What's holding you back?
5 What's already going well for you?
6 What question do you not want me to ask?
7 What question would you ask next?
8 What options do you have?
9 What will you do?
10 What has been most helpful to you in our conversation?

Cherie Silas:

1 What is the problem you are trying to solve?
2 If you had no impediments, what would you do?
3 Who can help with this?
4 What permission do you need to move forward?
5 What is happening in the culture/environment that may be contributing to this?
6 What is holding you back?
7 What is stopping you from doing "x" now?
8 What do you need to move forward?
9 What does your working agreement with "x" say about this?
10 What clarity is needed about roles and responsibilities?

Christine Thompson:

1 What needs to happen?
2 What's the new awareness?
3 How do you feel about saying that?
4 Why is that a problem for you?
5 Why is that important to you?
6 What's the smallest step you could take from here?
7 What are you learning?

Erkan Kadir:

1 What would you like to have happen? (Oftentimes coaching conversations start with a problem. While helping the client explore how they feel about an issue will help them to feel heard enough to move forward, talking about the issue itself only helps to re-trigger them back into the original trauma of the situation. This question serves the client by helping them move from the past to a positive future.)
2 What do we need to discuss in order to get you there? (I love this question because it puts the client into the driver seat and invites them to co-create the process we use. It keeps me humble when I otherwise might assume that I know what process is best for the client.)
3 What are you aware of? (This is a "blank access question," which invites the client into awareness without limiting them to a specific channel. The client might notice a new idea, a sensation in their body, a connection to a metaphor, or sights and sounds from their surrounding environment. Blank access questions expand possibilities and help the client exhaust information from the channel they're currently in without me presupposing where they should be drawing inspiration from. After all information from the current channel is exhausted, I'll invite the client to explore the issue from another.)
4 What stories are you making up about that? (This question helps the client explore the quality of their thinking. Often they're not aware of how much they have been thinking about an issue or how their current thinking might be limiting possibilities and getting in their way. There's also some great education built in to this question that serves to remind the client that the story in their head is just one of many perspectives.)
5 What would your hero/best future self/boss/best friend/mentor do? (I ask this question a lot because the answer for clients is oftentimes obvious and helps them to access their highest levels of consciousness.)
6 What else? (This is my favorite question. It always helps the client dig a little deeper and uncover even more information that they didn't know they had. I also use this question to focus back on my client in the event that I notice I'm stuck in my own head thinking about what question to ask next.)

Harris Christopoulos:

1   What's on your mind today?
2   If you had a magic wand, what would you change about your current situation?
3   What is stopping you from reaching your potential?
4   What would your future self tell you about your current situation?
5   How would your ideal day/situation look?

Kathy Suave:

1   On a scale of 1 to 10, how are you feeling right now about being able to do this? (I then check in later in the session to see how they're feeling.)
2   My follow-up question is: What are you doing now that helps you to be at that point? (I use this to draw out the positive.)
3   If you're saying yes to this, what are you unintentionally saying no to?
4   Where does this fit within your circle of control? (If they know what that means.)
5   What's the first step that you can take this week to get started?
6   Who can give you support or encouragement?

Mauricio Robles:

I try to avoid sticking to a set of questions, just to make sure that I'm not applying a "coaching formula." However, there are some areas I regularly explore during a coaching session:

1   Feelings: I try to use questions that help me mirror back to the client the feelings that he/she is going through:
   a   How do you feel when you talk about this?
   b   Can you describe what you are feeling right now?
   c   Which actions trigger this feeling?
2   Explore success: Help the customer visualize success
   a   What will success look like once you achieve the goal?
   b   What will make this conversation successful?
   c   If you have any resource at your disposal, where would you be?
3   Ownership
   a   Where would you like to start from now on?
   b   Which of these options do you have total control of?
   c   How would you like to hold yourself accountable?
   d   What can you do with these (options, actions, or ideas) that depend on someone else?

Miriam Cheuk:

Questions depend on the context. Instructional coaching requires very different questions than life/leadership coaching. I do different types of coaching conversations: planning, problem-solving, and reflecting conversations, so it all varies.

1   What are your non-negotiables?
2   What do you REALLY, REALLY want?
3   In a year (or whatever amount of time), what might you want to be able to say that you can't say now?
4   What are you telling yourself? / How do you know that to be true? / How do you challenge your own assumptions? / If limiting beliefs were not an issue, what might you be able to do?
5   If you had a magic wand (or a miracle could happen), what would that look like?
6   What are you pretending not to know?
7   What are you tolerating?
8   What haven't I asked you that I should ask you?
9   What aren't you telling me? / What else would be helpful for me to know?
10 What's the real issue? / What keeps you up at night?
11 If you were to write a book, what would be its title? / What would the book be about?
12 What would the relationship need from you?
13 How is this serving you? / What is this costing you? / What's at stake?
14 What are you not capitalizing on right now?
15 If nothing changes, what happens?
16 Who must you be right now to get (whatever you want)?
17 What would be possible if nothing held you back?
18 As you reflect on what you want to do, what is driving your thoughts?
19 What is your inkling? / If you did know, what would the answer be?
20 What's your signature presence?
21 What do you want your legacy to be?

Richard Lister:

In terms of internal coaching, there is a need to establish links with the wider system with questions such as:

1   If your line manager/the CEO was here, what would they say?
2   How would this idea *fit with* the organization's vision and priorities?
3   Can you see any tension between your personal goal here and the organization's?
4   How would this idea *contribute to* the organization's vision and priorities?

Vernon Stinebaker:

1 "And what else?" (The AWE question from *The Coaching Habit* by Michael Bungay Stanier.)
2 What are you taking away (from this session/topic)?
3 What about this is important to you?
4 What do *you* want?
5 How are you going to use this?
6 Please tell me more.

Viktur Glinka:

1 What experience did you get?
2 What will you do to get a different experience?
3 How will you use your experience?
4 What have you learned about yourself during our work?
5 How will you act now?

Questions for coaches to ask themselves

Val Hastings:

1   Who coaches me?
2   On a scale of 1 to 10 (1 = poor, 10 = outstanding), how good am I at remaining neutral?
3   How can I highlight what I'm noticing without making it good vs. bad, or right vs. wrong?
4   What is going well in the current way that I am working?
5   How ready is this person (team) to be coached?
6   What is my role today, right here, right now?
7   Who is my client? Who are my clients?
8   What's it like to be in a conversation with me?
9   What does the system need from me as the coach?
10 What do I need from the system to make this successful?
11 What is the client's agenda that I'm here to work on?

Viktur Glinka:

1 How do I feel right now? Am I in the right shape for coaching?
2 What do I want to notice about this coaching session?
3 What have I learned?
4 What would I do differently?
5 What opportunities do I see?

Questions to ask clients, to demonstrate the value of coaching

Val Hastings:

1 How much of this would you attribute to coaching?
2 What kind of value would you place on the coaching you have received? (1 = no value, 10 = high value)
3 How close did we get to meeting your objectives?
4 How would you rate yourself in this area? How would you rate your team in this area? (Ask this question before any coaching begins, and then again at the mid-point and at the end of the coaching agreement.)
5 (Question for myself as the coach) How will I use this data to demonstrate the value of coaching?

Managing an internal coaching team

Richard Lister:

Keep an internal database or register of anyone who has coaching or mentoring skills, or who you have invested in with coaching or mentoring skills.

The register should note, probably in bands, the amount of training they have, the number of coaching hours they have, their level of leadership experience, hours per month of availability, and particular strengths/experience (we know the iceberg tips of this and tend to forget all that people brought from previous work).

To be formally recognized as an internal coach, I recommend they have a level of experience/training. This comes with opportunities to use your skills, and potential coaching development input, but also standards such as the ICF code of ethics. As well, require that the coaches have a certain level of availability (i.e., hours).

The process for becoming such a coach should involve at least one observed coaching session with an experienced coach. Make the most of more experienced coaches to invest in less experienced ones with active learning or co-coaching sets.

17 Conclusion and suggested next steps

As a veteran coach trainer, my favorite part has been responding to the questions of new coaches—and I thought I had heard them all.

But I was proved wrong, after teaching a coaching class that included a number of internal coaches. A whole new series of questions began to surface, with one thing in common: internal coaching.

Looking back at my answers, I had made a number of assumptions about internal coaching that have been completely dispelled through the process of interviewing internal coaches for this book.

I believe I also dispelled some assumptions for some of the coaches themselves, primarily the idea that they were somehow not a "real" coach. Internal coaching IS coaching—100%! That being said, there are unique distinctions between external and internal coaching, which we explored with our guiding principles of internal coaching.

In addition to the dispelling of my assumptions, I have also discovered a unique opportunity for coaching. Organizations and businesses benefit immensely from internal coaching, especially having coaching living in their mess.

There are several learnings for me from writing this book, the following three of which stand out:

1 The importance of coaching the system. While there is value in coaching an individual, team, or group, we invariably fall short if the system remains unaffected. These unaffected systems, which were once thriving and healthy, soon become stale and even toxic. The system, like any other living organism, attempts to get our attention. Coaching the system is one significant way to notice and give voice to the system.

2 The valuable contribution of "switching hats" during the coaching conversation. As an external coach, I have been quite proud of the fact that I can stay in my role as coach almost 100% of the time—rarely needing to "switch hats." Those I have interviewed for this book have helped me appreciate the value—and yes, absolute need at times—to be directive and shift back and forth from one role to another, for the benefit of my clients.

3 The ongoing need to demonstrate your worth—for both internal and external coaches. Earlier in this book I mentioned that, as an external coach, I spend about 30% of my time demonstrating my worth, which in turns keeps my pipeline full. A huge assumption that I have had is that internal coaches

have a ready supply of clients and have no need to demonstrate their worth. As I have since discovered, nothing could be further from the truth. The reality is, if you're a coach, you have to be intentional about helping people understand what coaching is and why they should work with a coach.

What were your biggest learnings from reading this book?

Your next steps as an internal coach:

1 Put in place the guiding principles of internal coaching. Which are you already doing? Which need to be added? Which do you find the most challenging?
2 Consider additional training or working with a coach, mentor-coach, or supervising coach (see resources below).
3 Create your own community of practice with other internal coaches.

Internal coaching resources from Coaching4Today'sLeaders

Coach training

Our *Professional Coach Training* program equips leaders and professional coaches with the skills to be an effective coach, develop a coaching culture, and use a coaching approach in all aspects of leadership. In addition, this program will look at how to develop a coaching practice either internally in an organization or externally as a coaching professional.

Coaching is about getting results by bringing out the best in individuals, teams, and organizations. Coaching isn't about fixing or solving problems; rather, coaching is a developmental or discovery-based process that promotes development and sustained results. Similar to athletic coaches, coaches further develop the skill and talent already inherent in the individuals, teams, and organizations they coach.

An enormous benefit of coach training for leaders and professional coaches is that, as part of the training process, leaders and professional coaches receive their own coaching. That means dedicated one-on-one time to speak openly about challenges, goals, and outcomes. It means having someone else who is committed and able to draw out the best in YOU, so you are showing up at the top of YOUR game. This is a great opportunity to have support for your own development and solidify your coaching skills at the same time!

Coaching4Today'sLeaders offers 136 coach-specific training hours which can lead to the ACC, PCC, and MCC credentials if desired. Our Professional Coach Training program is offered in two formats: online distance learning and on-site/in-person training events.

Our program is designed to fit the needs of anyone who wishes to add coaching to their skillset, whether you are seeking foundational coaching skills or pursuing a coaching credential.

Customized internal coaching program

Invite Coaching4Today'sLeaders to develop an internal coaching program in your organization or business, including coach training. We will provide you with an all-inclusive ICF-accredited coach training program—and we will customize it to meet your specific needs and goals.

This training can be done in-person or online and includes coaching, coach training, and mentor-coaching. We currently facilitate coach training in six different languages: English, Spanish, French, Portuguese, Korean, and Ukrainian.

Visit https://coaching4todaysleaders.com/ to learn more or get started.

Bibliography

Bradberry, T. and Greaves, J. (2009) *Emotional Intelligence 2.0*, San Diego, CA: TalentSmart.

Kline, N. (2015) *More Time to Think: The Power of Independent Thinking*, London: Octopus Publishing.

Lencioni, P. (2002) *The Five Dysfunctions of a Team: A Leadership Fable*, San Francisco, CA: Jossey-Bass.

O'Neill, M.B. (2007) *Executive Coaching with Backbone and Heart: A Systems Approach to Engaging Leaders with Their Challenges*, 2nd edition, San Francisco, CA: Jossey-Bass.

Park, H.Y. (2000) *Develop Intercultural Competence*, Nashville, TN: General Board of Higher Education and Ministry.

Patterson, K., Grenny, J., McMillan, R. and Switzler, J. (2002) *Crucial Conversations: Tools for Talking When Stakes Are High*, 2nd edition, New York: McGraw-Hill Education.

Pedrick, C. (2020) *Simplifying Coaching: How to Have More Transformational Conversations by. Doing Less*, London: Open University Press.

Phillips, P.P., Phillips, J.J. and Edwards, L.A. (2012) *Measuring the Success of Coaching: A Step-by-Step Guide for Measuring Impact and Calculating ROI*, Alexandria, VA: ASTD Press.

Rutherford, A. (2019) *Learn to Think in Systems*, Dorottya Zita Varga Publisher.

Rutherford, A. (2019) *The Systems Thinker*, Dorottya Zita Varga Publisher.

Seligman, M.E.P. (1998) Building human strength: Psychology's forgotten mission, *APA Monitor*, January, p. 2.

Simpson, M. (2014) *Unlocking Potential: 7 Coaching Skills that Transform Individuals, Teams and Organizations*, Grand Haven, MI: Grand Harbor Press.

Singh Ospina, N., Phillips, K.A., Rodriguez-Gutierrez, R., Castaneda-Guarderas, A., Gionfriddo, M.R., Branda, M.E. and Montori, V.M. (2019) Eliciting the patient's agenda—secondary analysis of recorded clinical encounters, *Journal of General Internal Medicine*, 34 (1): 36–40.

Stanier, M.B. (2016) *The Coaching Habit: Say Less, Ask More & Change the Way You Lead Forever*, Vancouver: Page Two.

Titelman, P. (2008) *Triangles: Bowen Family Systems Theory Perspectives*, New York: Haworth Press.

Tkach, J.T. and DiGirolamo, J.A. (2017) The state and future of coaching supervision, *International Coaching Psychology Review*, 12 (1): 49–63.

Zander, R.S. and Zander, B. (2006) *The Art of Possibility*, London: Penguin Books.

Index